I0119851

Oscar Tully Shuck

Historical Abstract of San Francisco

Vol. 1

Oscar Tully Shuck

Historical Abstract of San Francisco
Vol. 1

ISBN/EAN: 9783744662987

Printed in Europe, USA, Canada, Australia, Japan

Cover: Foto ©ninafisch / pixelio.de

More available books at **www.hansebooks.com**

CITY HALL.

HISTORICAL ABSTRACT

OF

SAN FRANCISCO

PREPARED AND PUBLISHED BY

OSCAR T. SHUCK

AUTHOR OF "BENCH AND BAR IN CALIFORNIA"

AND OF

"REPRESENTATIVE MEN OF THE PACIFIC."

IN THREE VOLUMES
Vol. I.

SAN FRANCISCO
1897.

To

Col. Daniel M. Burns,

First Secretary of State under the present Constitution, I beg leave, while he is far away in "Our Sister Republic," to inscribe this first volume of a history of the great city of which he is a distinguished citizen.

THE AUTHOR.

INTRODUCTORY

In the years close to the middle of the century, when, being connected with the press, I began to watch the current of events in the local world, the habit was formed of preserving notes of all that claimed the eye, as an aid in miscellaneous writing. These, which inevitably became more and more manifold and engaging, were a faithful guide and stay through a long and active period, and they have been supplemented to date. They are now arranged, it is believed, in the most convenient form for reference, that of the alphabet, and are published as deserving perpetuity and possessing universal interest.

O. T. S.

San Francisco, Cal., May 1, 1897.

Much important matter and some notable names, passed over in Vol. I, for various reasons, will be found in the Supplement at the end of Vol. III.

CALIFORNIA ACADEMY OF SCIENCES

A

Abbotsford House, Broadway, was erected by Michael Brogan, (Thomas Turnbull, architect) in 1870, at a cost of $30,000, and was called the Parisian Hotel; name changed to Abbotsford in 1875.

Abbott, John E.; admitted to the bar in his native State, N. H.; came to California in 1858: settled in S. F. in 1882; Supervisor for the 4th Ward 1885-86; chairman of the judiciary committee; during this period he was counsel for Mrs. Hannah Ingram in her litigation with her husband, and was shot by the latter and seriously wounded; in the spring of 1887 bought a residence at Mountain View and embarked in agriculture; was there mortally injured by a runaway horse, and died Nov. 16, 1887, aged 54.

Abell, Alexander G.; pioneer of Nov. 6, 1847: prominent Mason; State Senator, 14th session, 1863; registered as a voter Aug. 8, 1867, as a native of N. Y., aged 47; was Grand Secretary of Free and Accepted Masons 1855-90; was President of the Pioneers for three terms, 1857-60; died Dec. 28, 1890.

Abell, William H.; a prisoner in the dock of the Police Court, suddenly drew a razor and cut his throat, inflicting a mortal wound, April 2, 1868.

Academy of Languages, (De Filippe's) was established in 1871.

Academy of Medicine, (California) was organized Sept. 26, 1891.

Academy of Sciences, (California) was organized April 4, 1853; was presented with its valuable Market street lot by James Lick, Sept. 24, 1875.

Acheson, Thos. S.; Supervisor, 1878-79; office declared vacant by the Board of Supervisors, Nov. 10, 1879.

Acker, Nicholas A.; born in Washington, D. C., March 20, 1864; admitted to the bar there, in 1887; located in San Francisco in 1889, and has since made patent law a specialty.

Ackerson, C. H.; Second Assistant Engineer Fire Department 1867 to July 20, 1870; Chief Engineer July 20, 1870, to April 4, 1871.

Ackerson, Wm. W.; Superintendent of Streets, 1893-1894.

Adams, A. C.; was judge of the Eleventh judicial district comprising El Dorado, Amador and Calaveras Counties, for the year 1869, appointed to fill a vacancy; was elected for a full term of six years beginning January, 1870; removed to S. F. in 1876; was born in Penn., March 3, 1824.

Adams, Charles A.; son of the last named by his second marriage, was born at Mokelumne Hill, Calaveras Co., Cal., Nov. 25, 1867 Removed to S. F. in 1876, graduated from University of California in 1887, and later from Hastings College of the Law. On January 14, 1889, was admitted to the Supreme Court of California. In Feb. 1891, he entered into law partnership with his father, under the firm name of Adams & Adams.

Adams, Edwin, made his first appearance at the California Theater, Oct. 4, 1869.

Adams, Rev. Geo. C., formally installed as pastor of First Congregational Church, as successor of Rev. Dr. Chas. O. Brown, Sunday, Dec. 27, 1896.

Adams, James; Supervisor, 1870-71; Sheriff, 1872-73.

Adams, John Quincy; born in N. J., June 27, 1844; came in infancy to S. F., arriving March 26, 1847, with his father, a member of "Stevenson's Regiment;" educated in the S. F. public schools, and in the Collegiate Institute, and Law College, Benicia; admitted to the bar of the State Supreme Court, Oct. 13, 1873; delivered the Annual Oration before the Society of California Pioneers (of which he is a member) in Sept., 1872.

Adams & Co., leading bankers, suspended Feb. 23, 1855. Alfred A. Cohen, receiver, was succeeded by Gen. Henry M. Naglee.

Addis, John; Street Commissioner, Oct. 1853—Oct. 1854.

Addison, Gen. John E.; the first County Clerk (1850), who had been a great sufferer from gout, fearing another attack, committed suicide Sept. 3, 1874; registered as a voter July 31, 1867, as a native of Virginia, lawyer, aged 47. A pioneer of Oct. 29, 1849.

Addison, William A., was found dead in his room (an apoplectic fit), May 29, 1875.

Adelphi Theater, erected on Dupont St., bet. Clay and Washington, by members of the theatrical profession, was opened in July, 1851. John Lewis Baker became manager May 9, 1853.

Admission of California as a State of the Union; news reached S. F. by steamer Oregon from Panama, Oct. 18, 1850. Public celebration Oct. 29th; procession; oration by Judge Nathaniel Bennett; ball at the California Exchange. Same day, boiler of steamboat Saginaw burst at the wharf, killing 30 persons.

Advent Sunday School Chapel, corner stone laid January 18, 1868.

Aeronaut, Captain Barbiere, arrived with the French Mail Balloon, Le Secours, March 20, 1874; made his first ascension from Woodward's Gardens, March 28th.

Affrays: The most desperate shooting affray of local record, was between Will Hicks Graham and Geo. Frank Lemon (familiar names of old) at the Union Hotel, corner Kearny and Merchant streets, July 3, 1851; they fought a duel later: see Duels.

Hon. Delos Lake, Judge Fourth District Court, assaulted Sanderson Davidson, of the Weekly Leader, for alleged libel in that paper, Oct. 30, 1854; pleaded "guilty of cruelty to animals," and paid a fine of $50.

For the battle between Eugene Casserly, distinguished lawyer, and McKean Buchanan, tragedian, see local press, Oct. 17, 1855.

Street encounter between John G. Downey, Governor of the State, John Middleton, leading auctioneer, and Myles D. Sweeny, President Hibernia Bank, about politics (all prominent Douglas Democrats), July 15, 1861.

George Barstow, Speaker of the Assembly, physically assaulted by R. D. Ferguson, Assemblyman from Sacramento, in the temporary Capitol building (the legislature having adjourned from Sacramento on account of the great flood), April 9, 1862. (Ferguson afterwards became Speaker of the Nevada Assembly.)

Shots were exchanged between Don Carlos Butterfield and John Sevenoaks, Dec. 14, 1877.

Between Gustavus de Young, of the Chronicle, and F. R. Fitzgerald, of the Sun, Jan. 31, 1874.

The Sun-Chronicle troubles broke out anew—Chas. de Young shot at Ben Napthaly, June 16, 1874.

Street encounter between R. M. Daggett and Calvin B. McDonald, Sept. 24, 1861. D. was afterwards U. S. Minister to Hawaii; McD. was a noted editor.

Col. A. Andrews assaulted Geo. Thistleton for alleged libel in the "Jolly Giant," Nov. 9, 1876.

Shooting between J. Eisner and H. Robitschek in regard to business matters, resulted in the death of Eisner and the wounding of Robitschek, Dec. 27, 1867. R. was tried and acquitted.

Chas. de Young was assaulted by John Duane, Oct. 21, 1876.

Geo. K. Fitch was assaulted on the street by R. R. Campbell, Ex-State Registrar, with a cowhide, Dec. 14, 1860; F. vigorously checkmated his disturber.

For Captain Chadwick's assault on Capt. Lees, see Sacramento Union (telegram), Dec. 21, 1860.

Wm. H. Dow and Wm. G. Badger, prominent merchants and members of Calvary Presbyterian Church, had trouble over their pastor during the war of the rebellion; D., a friend of Rev. Dr. W. A. Scott, struck B., was convicted of battery, and forfeited his bail, June 5, 1862.

Shots were exchanged between Thos. Maguire, John H. Burns, of the Snug Saloon, and John A. Crabtree, Dec. 20, 1863; C., who was father to the since renowned actress Lotta, was convicted of assault with deadly weapon, March 16, 1864.

Set-to between Hon. Robert Ferral, then Judge of the City Criminal Court, and Geo. W. Tyler, prominent lawyer, occurred in the former's Court room, March 31, 1877.

Agassiz, Prof. Louis, and party, arrived Aug. 31, 1872.

Aitken, John R.; prominent lawyer; born in S. F., March 31, 1854; graduate of Hastings Law College; admitted to the bar of the Supreme Court, June 10, 1886; removed to San Diego in 1888, and elected Superior Judge to succeed John D. Works, resigned; filled out the fractional term ending Dec. 31, 1888; returned to S. F. in 1893.

Aimée Opera Troupe first appeared at the California Theater, May 18, 1874

Air Navigation; an aerial steamer was successfully tested by an ascension at the City Gardens, Jan. 14, 1871.

Alaska was formally transferred to the United States, Oct. 18, 1867; Capt. Peteschawroff acting as Commissioner for Russia, and Brevet Maj. Gen. Rousseau for the U. S. News thereof was received at S. F. Nov. 14, 1867.

First regular mail was dispatched by steamer Oct. 18, 1869.

Steamer John L. Stephens sailed September 25, 1867, being the first of a line of steamers established between this State and the recently acquired territory; Gen. Jefferson C. Davis, Military Commander of Alaska, and other army officers, were passengers.

Steamer Ossipee sailed for Alaska Sept. 27, 1867, having on board Gen. Rousseau and Staff and the Russian Commissioners.

Rivers of Alaska; Article by John Muir in S. F. Bulletin, Jan. 20, 1880.

Interesting collection of Aleutian mummies was received at the warehouse of the Alaska Commercial Co., Jan. 9, 1875.

Alcaldes of San Francisco after the American occupation: A. D. 1846, W. A. Bartlett; 1847, Edwin Bryant; succeeded by Geo. Hyde; 1848, J. Townsend; succeeded by T. M. Leavenworth; 1849, John W. Geary.

Alcazar Building and Theater; owned and built by M. H. de Young, was completed early in 1885.

Alcatraz Island; barracks were destroyed by fire April 19, 1874; Alcatraz Island has an area of 35 acres.

Alden, James; Rear Admiral U. S. N., died Feb. 6, 1877.

Aldrich, Lewis; pioneer of Sept. 18, 1849; early District Judge of Sacramento; brother-in-law of Hon. Wm. M. Stewart and Hon. W. W. Foote; died at S. F. May 19, 1885, native of R. I., aged 65. Decided the case of People vs. Geo. K. Fitch; see Cal. Supreme Court Reports, vol. I, page 520.

Alemany, Joseph Sadoc; arrived at S. F. in July, 1850; was Catholic Archbishop of S. F. from 1853 to May, 1885. Departed by steamer on a visit to the Papal See, April 30, 1867. Bought of David Mahoney, Oct. 4 1869, 300 acres of land near Lake Merced, for cemetery purposes. Made a second visit to Rome in 1870, returning Nov. 15th. Citizens celebrated the 25th anniversary of his transfer to this diocese, July 29, 1875. He returned to his native province, Valencia, Spain, and died there, April 8, 1888. Was born in 1812, and came to the U. S. in 1847.

Alexander, Barton Stone, Gen. U. S. A., President of Board of Engineers of the Pacific Coast, died at S. F. Dec. 15, 1878; native of Kentucky; aged 57.

Alexander, Daniel E.; well known lawyer of Sacramento, where he settled in 1850 and in later years held public offices; Democratic candidate for Superior Judge in 1879; removed to S. F., May 29, 1888, and returned to the Capital City in 1890; was born in Miss., Feb. 7,

1845, and admitted to the bar of the California Supreme Court, Feb. 7, 1866. Brother of Ex-Judge John K. Alexander of Monterey County.

Alexander, Eli; Veteran of Waterloo, died Nov. 16, 1870.

Alexander, John K.; Superior Judge of Monterey County, and a member of the S. F. Bar Association, received the degree of LL. D. from the Los Angeles University July 25, 1888.

Alhambra Theater, Bush Street; corner stone laid with appropriate ceremonies, Feb. 13, 1868; was first opened to the public, May 22, 1868.

Allen, James M.; Superior Judge, 1880-82; Presiding Judge in the last year.

Almshouse, The; was first opened for the reception of patients, Sept. 12, 1867.

Alsip, Edwin K.; old citizen and real estate operator of Sacramento, removed to S. F. in 1891, since which year he has been prominent in the same line; author of an article, "The Financial Problem," in S. F. Examiner, Aug. 8, 1893.

Alsup, J. R., native of Memphis, Tenn., aged 26, a prisoner on the ship Valparaiso from Chile, jumped from the ship into the bay, Oct. 7, 1879, and escaped; history of his previous capture and of his embezzlement, in press of Oct. 8, 1879.

Alvarado, Juan B., Governor of California, under Mexican rule, 1836-43. Died at San Pablo, July 13, 1882; born at Monterey, Cal., in 1809; sketch in "Representative Men."

Alvord, William; Mayor, and President Board of Health, 1872-73; Park Commissioner 1874-78, and 1882-83; Police Commissioner since 1878; President of the Pacific Rolling Mills Co. 1874-92; President of Bank of California since 1879.

American Bank and Trust Company of S. F. was incorporated Dec. 7, 1887.

Americus Club, of New York City, arrived on a tour of the State, May 3, 1871.

American Legion of Honor; Grand Council of California was instituted Aug. 8, 1881.

American Sugar Refinery; succeeded, in 1879, to the property and business of the Bay Refinery, which had been established 1864; a new company was formed, the American Sugar Refinery Company, with a paid up capital of $1,000,000 in 1885; the property was purchased by Havemeyers & Elder, N. Y., in March, 1889; cost, $1,250,000.

American Tract Society; Pacific Agency was established Dec., 1869.

Ames, Fisher, was born in N. H., Feb. 8, 1844; educated at Dartmouth College; admitted to the bar at Albany, N. Y., May 10, 1870, and came to S. F. same year; School Director 1876-77; Democratic candidate for City and County Attorney, Nov. 1884; member of the Board of Freeholders, elected to frame a City Charter, 1882; Fire Commissioner, 1887-92.

Ames, Capt. Henry; old resident, was run over by a truck on Davis street, and killed, Aug. 13, 1867.

Ames, John W.; U. S. Surveyor General at S. F.; appointed Sept. 24, 1877; died in office, April 6, 1878.

Ames, Pelham W.; born in Mass., April 22, 1839; educated at Harvard
College; Assistant paymaster U. S. N., 1861-66; located in S. F. in
March, 1872, and was admitted to the bar, March 21, 1884; Secre-
tary Sutro Tunnel Co., 1873-90; School Director, 1893-94; Assistant
Secretary Spring Valley Water Works since 1890.

An Afternoon of Blood; Billy Mulligan, in delirium tremens, fatally shot
his friend Jack McNabb, also John Hart, foreman of Eureka Hose
Co., from the balcony of the St. Francis Hotel, S. W. Clay and
Dupont Streets; and was himself shot dead by the police after
several attempts to capture him, July 7, 1865.

Ancient Order of Foresters; subsidiary High Court of the Pacific Coast
was instituted in S. F., Nov. 6, 1889.

Ancient Order of United Workmen; Grand Lodge of California was organized, Nov. 17, 1877; Grand Lodge of the Degree of Honor was organized, May 25, 1893.

Anderson, Dr. Jerome A.; Member of Board of Freeholders, which framed
the proposed Charter defeated at the general election, Nov. 3, 1896;
prominent physician.

Anderson, James W.; Superintendent of Common Schools, S. F., 1887-90;
State Superintendent, 1891-94.

Anderson & Randolph's Jewelry Store was robbed of a large amount of
jewelry, Jan. 30, 1870.

"Andrew Jackson," clipper ship, arrived from New York in 89 days—
beating the famous passage of the clipper ship Flying Cloud by 6
hours— March 24, 1860.

Andros, Milton; distinguished lawyer; was born in Mass.; admitted to
the bar of the U. S. Supreme Court, in Dec., 1855; Assistant U. S.
Attorney for Mass., 1857-61; located in S. F., Dec. 2, 1865; was attorney for P. M. S. S. Co. for some years; the partnership existing
between him and Nathan H. Frank was formed in 1889.

Animals, Society to Prevent Cruelty to, was incorporated April, 1868.
Act of the legislature for the Prevention of cruelty to Animals,
was approved March 30, 1868.

Anglo-Californian Bank, Limited, (S. F. Branch) was incorporated April 5,
1873; bought the lot N. E. corner Pine and Sansome, for $175,000,
Sept. 10, 1881.

Anthony, James; head of the long powerful company, founders of
the Sacramento Union; a veteran of the Mexican War; pioneer of Aug. 30, 1849; died at S. F., Jan. 5, 1876; native of Penn.,
aged 52. The legislature being in session, adjourned in honor of
his memory.

Anti-Coolie Convention assembled July 5, 1877.

Appalling accident at the Oakland Ferry, on the Oakland side, July 4,
1868; the breaking of a gang plank precipitated over 100 persons
into the water, about 20 lives being lost.

Appraisers' Building (U. S. Customs) Sansome, Washington and Jackson
streets; construction was begun in May, 1873; completed, and
building turned over to T. B. Shannon, Collector of the Port, Jan.

30, 1880; cost, $800,000; saved the Government $40,000 per annum in rents.

"Archy," slave boy, was remanded to the custody of his owner, C. A. Stovall, of Mississippi, by the State Supreme Court, Feb. 11, 1858; U. S. Commissioner Geo. Pen. Johnston discharged him on *habeas corpus*, as being a freeman, April 14, 1858; had been taken before Johnston, after having been released by County Judge Freelon, March 18, 1858.

Arctic Exploration; New York Herald Expedition; steam yacht Jeannette, started on her voyage at 4 P. M. Tuesday, July 8, 1879; De Long, commander.

Ariel Rowing Club was organized April 17, 1877; incorporated Feb. 15, 1887.

Argenti, Felix; pioneer banker, died May 19, 1861.

Arsenic; a Miss Cook died from effects of, taken to beautify her complexion, April 26, 1869.

Art Association, The San Francisco; organized March 28, 1871, opening reception at their rooms, 430 Pine street, Feb. 8, 1877; incorporated July 30, 1889; School of Design was organized Dec. 31, 1873; name of the S. F. Art Association changed to Mark Hopkins Institute of Art in 1893; received as a gift same year from Edward F. Searles, the magnificent mansion and grounds on Nob Hill, which it has since occupied; the first of Mr. Searles' contributions of paintings to this Association was received at S. F. in July, 1893, Mr. S. further promising to give $5,000 a year to maintain the Gallery.

Arts, Mechanical, California School of, was founded by James Lick with an endowment of $540,000, and was incorporated in 1885.

Art Union, California; incorporated Nov. 1, 1864. Rooms at 312 Montgomery street opened with an elegant collation, Jan. 11, 1865.

Ashbury, James, distinguished yachtsman, of the Royal Thames Yacht Club, sent from England to the S. F. Yacht Club, a silver tankard and other presents, in return for courtesies received on his visit to the State; Aug. 24, 1871; arrived on his second visit, Aug. 29, 1876.

Ashbury, Monroe; Supervisor, 1864-70; member Board of Health, 1868-69; Auditor, 1871-75; defeated for Mayor by Andrew J. Bryant in 1877; prominent Odd Fellow; died May 4, 1886; native of Maryland, aged 62. At the election of Sept. 3, 1873, when he ran the second time for Auditor, there was only one vote against his total of 25,817.

Ashburner, Wm.; distinguished mining engineer; came to California in 1860, as one of the Chief Assistants in the State Geological Survey, under Prof. J. D. Whitney; one of the commissioners to manage Yosemite Valley and Mariposa Big Tree Grove, 1864-80; Professor of Mining in University of California, 1874; Honorary Professor of Mining, 1876; Regent, same University, 1880, to his death. One of the original 24 trustees of the Leland Stanford University; died at S. F., April 20, 1887, a native of Mass., aged 56 years; funeral from Trinity Episcopal Church; estate appraised, Aug. 18, 1887, at $30,188.

Ashe, Dr. R. P.; distinguished physician; was elected unanimously by the legislature Visiting Physician of the State Hospital at Stockton, April 29, 1851; Sheriff of San Joaquin County, 1851-52; pioneer of Aug. 20, 1849; died at S. F. Sept. 6, 1871; native of N. C., aged 48; R. Porter Ashe, well-known at the bar, and on the turf, since 1881, is a son of Dr. Ashe.

Ashley, Delos R., State Treasurer of California in 1862-63, and M. C. from Nevada, 1865-66; father-in-law of Daniel O'Connell, journalist and poet; died at S. F., July 18, 1873.

Ashworth, Thomas; Supervisor, 1883-84; Superintendent of Streets two terms, 1887-90; also Sup't Streets, Nov., Dec., 1886, vice Chas. S. Ruggles, deceased; same office 1895-96.

Associated Charities was organized in March, 1888.

Atherton, Faxon Dean; capitalist; pioneer of April 21, 1836, died at S. F., July 18, 1877.

Atlantic Cable Celebration, Sept. 27, 1858. (E. D. Baker's noble oration is the opening piece in the *California Scrap Book.*)

Atwood, Wm. T.; Secretary Board of Freeholders which framed the defeated City Charter of 1880.

Aurora Borealis caused a general alarm of fire, Sept. 6, 1860.

Aurora Light, a beautiful display, April 8, 1870; another grand display, Sept. 24, 1870.

Authors' Carnival at Mechanics' Pavilion, Oct. 23d to Nov. 6, 1879. The charitable societies benefitted were the Old Ladies' Home, Young Women's Christian Association, Clay Street Hospital, Infants' Shelter, and the Pacific Dispensary for Women and Children. These received $3,000 each, Oct. 28, 1879.

Austin, Alexander, former dry goods merchant, Tax Collector three terms, 1869-75, afterwards stock broker, died at his country home in San Mateo County, Sept. 11, 1878, native of Scotland, aged 56.

Austin, Joseph, brother of the preceding, Park Commissioner since 1886.

Australian and American Line of Steamships; the MacGregor, pioneer vessel of the line, arrived from Sidney, Jan. 25, 1874.

Australia; the P. M. S. S. Co. dispatched their first steamer on the Australian route, Nov. 10, 1875.

Avery, Benjamin Parke.; editor, literary and art critic, died while U. S. Minister to China, at Pekin, Nov. 8, 1875; native of N. Y., aged 47. Was State Printer, 1862-63; editor S. F. Evening Bulletin 1865-72; editor Overland Monthly, and Secretary Art Association, 1873; his remains were brought from China, and funeral was from First Unitarian Church, Jan. 26, 1876.

Axtell, Samuel B; Member of congress, two terms, March 4, 1867 – March 4, 1871; died in New Jersey, Aug. 7, 1891.

Ayer, Dr. Washington; pioneer of July 5, 1849; School Director, 1865-68; Supervisor, 1891-92; author of an article on "Sewer Gases and Disease," in Bulletin, Sept. 25, 1885.

Ayres, J. C.; landscape artist of S. F.; was lost with the schooner Laura Bevans, near San Pedro, May 10, 1858.

GERTRUDE ATHERTON.

B

Babcock, Henry S., Vice-President and Manager Security Savings Bank, died May 19, 1873; native of Louisiana, aged 45.

Babcock, Wm. F., of Parrott & Co., old and wealthy citizen, died Sept. 22, 1885; native of Massachusetts, aged 59; was President of Chamber of Commerce, 1875.

Baby Show at Pacific Hall, July 16, 1873. In Platt's Hall, Jan. 14, 1878, 150 babes contested for prizes.

Bacon, H. D.; wealthy real estate dealer; President Pacific Express, 1869-70; in 1878 donated $25,000 to the State University for a Library and Art Building; in April, 1878, the legislature appropriated a like sum to be added to Mr. B's donation and used for same purpose.

Backus, Samuel W.; a resident of S. F. since 1862; served in the war of the Rebellion; member of Assembly, 1877-78; Adjutant-General under Gov. Perkins, 1880-82; Postmaster under President Arthur for four years ending July 1, 1886; same under President Harrison for four years ending July 1, 1894; registered as a voter July 2, 1866, as a native of New York, aged 22.

Badlam, Alexander, Jr.; a pioneer of June 30, 1849; Member of Assembly from Sacramento, 1863-64; Member of Board of Health S. F., 1870; Supervisor, 1870-71; Assessor, 1875-82; registered as a voter June 16, 1866, as a native of Ohio, aged 30.

Badger, Mrs. Wm. G.; widely respected resident, died Sept. 16, 1871.

Badger, Wm. G.; School Director three terms, 1862-67; resigned April 30, 1867; registered as a voter June 11, 1866, as a native of Massachusetts, aged 42; prominent in the importing clothing and piano trade since the early Fifties. See Affrays.

Bagley, David T.; pioneer of Feb. 28, 1849; Public Administrator, 1851-52; registered as a voter July 25, 1867, as a native of Louisiana, aged 45.

Baggett, William Thomas; prominent lawyer, was born in Mississippi, Dec. 16, 1850; admitted to the bar in Tennessee in 1873; located in S. F. in 1877; in 1878, issued the *Pacific Coast Law Journal;* the following year published the S. F. *Law Journal* in association with F. A. Schofield; in 1880-81, owned the *Pacific Coast Law Journal* with Wm. H. Davis, also then edited the *Daily Examiner,* of which he was part owner; 1881-83, in association with Mr. Davis and Jas. H. Stockwell, owned and published the *Daily Law Journal,* which journal is still owned and conducted by him and Mr. S. At the bar in S. F., Mr. B. conducted the notable case of Fox vs. Hale & Norcross Mining Co. where his client, the plaintiff, obtained the largest money judgment ever rendered in a contested case in this State.

Bahrs, George H.; Judge Superior Court, elected Nov., 1894, for six years beginning Jan., 1895.

Bailey, Geo. W.; a lawyer of Benicia, for some time missing, remains found at Visitacion Valley, a pistol shot through the skull, Jan. 26, 1873.

Baird, Capt. John H.; President of California Powder Works, died at Palace Hotel, Nov. 12, 1880, native of Kentucky, aged 65; funeral from St. John Presbyterian Church; was State Senator, 1853.

Baker, Col. E. D., Chief Quartermaster of the Department of the Columbia, son of the celebrated orator whose full name he bore, died at Vancouver, W. T., Jan. 25, 1883, aged 44.

Baker, Edward D.; "The foremost man of all this (western) world," born in London, England, in 1811; came with his parents to the U. S. at the age of five; was a Major at 21 in the Black Hawk war; represented the Springfield, Illinois, district in Congress, 1845-46; was a Colonel in the war with Mexico; in Congress again, 1849-50; was Superintendent of Construction of the Panama Railroad, 1851; arrived in S. F. in June, 1852; was defeated for Congress on the Republican ticket in 1859; removed to Oregon, and was elected U. S. Senator in 1860; went into the war of the Rebellion, as a Colonel, while still holding his seat in the Senate, and fell in his first fight, at Ball's Bluff, Virginia, Oct. 21, 1861.

Baker's magnetic "American Theater speech" is in the City press of Oct. 28, 1860; his "Forest Hill" speech is reported in the Sacramento Union, August 23, 1859; his "Atlantic Cable Address" is in the "California Scrap Book;" his "Poem to a Wave," his Remarks at the funeral of Hon. Wm. I. Ferguson at Sacramento, 1858, and his masterpiece, the Oration at the burial of Broderick, S. F., 1859, are in "Representative Men of the Pacific." A sketch of this great orator, lawyer and soldier forms the opening chapter in "Bench and Bar in California."

Baker, Capt. Isaiah; died June 26, 1885; native of Mass.; funeral from First Baptist Church.

Baker, Isaac F.; special policeman; died from injuries received from overturning of a stage coach, Aug. 21, 1869.

Baker, Mary F.; recovered verdict against the California Stage Co., for $10,000 damages for the death of her husband, Sept. 20, 1870. Mary Grady, injured at same time, recovered $3,000.

Baker, Thomas C., after ten years' absence at Los Angeles, returned to S. F. in Nov., 1881, and found that his estate had been administered upon by Pub. Adm. Wm. Doolan. The probate proceedings were set aside.

Baldwin, Alexander White; U. S. District Judge for Nevada, son of Joseph G. Baldwin, was killed by a collision of trains on the Western Pacific R. R., seven miles East of Oakland, Nov. 14, 1869.

Baldwin, Barry; prominent real estate dealer; President Merchants' Exchange Association, 1889-91; President of the Traffic Association, 1891-94; appointed U. S. Marshal at S. F. by President Cleveland for four years from July 1, 1894, on which day he assumed the office; registered July 10, 1896, as born in Wales, aged 52.

Baldwin, E. J. (Lucky Baldwin); builder and owner of Baldwin Hotel; registered as a voter July 23, 1866: "Elias Jackson Baldwin, native of Ohio, age 41, real estate operator."

Baldwin, Jennie Violet, wife of E. J., died Nov. 16, 1881; native of S. F., aged 23.

Baldwin Hotel was leased by Henry H. Pearson Dec. 1, 1882, for five years at $3,000 per month the first year, $3,333.33 per month the second year, and $4,000 per month for balance of term.

Baldwin, Dr. John; was killed in an open lot on Greenwich street near Dupont, Aug. 1, 1853, by Joseph Hetherington, the same man who killed another physician, Dr. Andrew Randall, in 1856, and who was, with Philander Brace, hung by the Great Vigilance Committee, July 29, 1856.

Baldwin, Joseph G.; distinguished jurist; a precocious mind, born in Virginia, Jan. 22, 1815. Admitted to the bar in Alabama. In that State he won a great reputation as a lawyer, and also produced his two far-famed books, "Flush Times," and "Party Leaders." Came to California in 1854, locating in S. F. Judge B. died at S. F. Oct. 1, 1864, in his 50th year, that period in which (he had himself declared) the intellectual faculties reach the zenith of their power, splendor and usefulness. A chapter is devoted to his life in "Bench and Bar in California."

It was Baldwin (not yet a judge) who said of the Supreme Court decision in the "Archy Case" (1858): "It gives the law to the North, and the nigger to the South." (See Bench and Bar in California, page 277.)

Baldwin, Loyd; prominent lawyer; was born in Maine; a graduate of Union College, N. Y., located in S. F. in 1862; Professor of the English language in the Academic Seminary, Rev. Elkan Cohn, principal, 1863; admitted to the bar in 1866. He died in Oakland, Oct. 19, 1885, aged 45, and left to his widow, a niece of D. J. Staples, an estate appraised at $45,000. He was a Unitarian.

Ball, A. Everett; born in N. Y., Oct. 28, 1845, educated at the Arcade Academy and at the University of Michigan; admitted to the bar in March, 1869, and located in S. F. in 1870; practiced with Judge E. D. Sawyer for twelve years, and thereafter alone; is connected with many business enterprises.

Ballinger, Frank J.; well-known "Call" reporter; died in 1885; native of Mass., aged 33.

Bancroft, Mrs. A. A.; mother of H. H. and A. L. Bancroft, died at Nordhoff, Cal., March 21, 1885; native of Mass., aged 86 years.

Bancroft, H. H.; historian; registered Aug. 6, 1869, as born in Ohio, aged 36; his residence, S. W. corner California and Franklin streets, was built in 1870; cost $50,000; located in Cambridge, Mass. in 1895.

Bancroft, H. H. & Co.; booksellers and stationers at 609 Montgomery street

from the early Fifties; removed to their own building on Market
street, and style changed to A. L. Bancroft & Co., in 1870; Bancroft-Whitney Co., 1887; same, also The Bancroft Company, 1888;
so continuing to date, the Bancroft Company being publishers, the
Bancroft-Whitney Co. being law publishers and stationers; while
the style of A. L. Bancroft & Co. (incorporated) is borne (1888-97)
by a house holding agencies for pianos and organs.

Bancroft Building; Market street, between 3rd and 4th, 75x170, extending
to Stevenson street, was erected 1869-70; cost $120,000; was nearly
destroyed by fire in 1886.

"Bankers, Private;" interesting article in Bulletin of March 24, 1887; slight
correction by Joseph A. Donohoe, same paper next day.

Bank of British Columbia (S. F. Branch), was incorporated by royal charter, 1862.

Bank of British North America was incorporated by royal charter, 1840.

Bank of California incorporated June 16, 1864; capital, $2,000,000; opened
for business S. W. corner Battery and Washington streets, July 1,
1864; removed to its own new building, N. W. California and Sansome streets, June 27, 1866; suspended Aug. 26, 1875; syndicate
organized with Wm. Sharon as president, Sept. 25, 1875, and bank
resumed business amid general rejoicing, Oct. 2, 1875; re-incorporated Dec. 2, 1875; reduced interest to one per cent. per month,
Dec. 12, 1876.

Bank of Commerce was incorporated May 24, 1895.

Bank of San Francisco wound up its business, Jan. 26, 1878, (N. P. Cole,
President; Horatio McPherson, cashier; J. L. Brown, manager).

Banks, Savings; California Savings and Loan Society was incorporated
June 24, 1873.

    Columbus Savings and Loan Society was incorporated Jan.
18, 1893.

    French Savings and Loan Society, (Gustave Mahe's) was in-
corporated, Feb. 1, 1860; suspended, Sept. 18, 1878.

    French Savings and Loan Society was incorporated March 11,
1879 (California street).

    German Savings and Loan Society was incorporated Feb. 10,
1868.

    Hibernia Savings and Loan Society was incorporated April 12,
1859.

    Humboldt Savings and Loan Society was incorporated Nov.
24, 1869.

    Masonic Savings and Loan Society, incorporated Nov. 4, 1869,
went into liquidation in 1879.

    Mutual Savings Bank of San Francisco was incorporated Nov.
21, 1889.

    Odd Fellows Savings Bank was incorporated Oct. 13, 1866; in
liquidation since March 1, 1880.

    Pioneer Land and Loan Bank (Duncan's) was incorporated in
April, 1869; failed Oct. 7, 1877.

San Francisco Savings Union was incorporated June 18, 1862.

Savings and Loan Society, the first Savings Bank established and whose name, therefore, is unfortunately not distinctive, was incorporated July 23, 1857; re-incorporated Dec. 12, 1865.

Security Savings Bank was incorporated, March 2, 1881.

"Bannock Mines" attracted general notice in the Spring of 1864.

Baptists dedicated the first Protestant Church, August 5, 1849.

Baptist Churches, the "Tabernacle" and "Columbia Square" united under the name of the Metropolitan Baptist Church, with I. S. Kalloch (afterwards Mayor) as pastor, March 3, 1875.

Baptist Church edifice on North side Washington street, East of Stockton, was purchased by Chinamen, for mercantile and lodging uses, May 28, 1875.

Baptist Church, First; on Eddy street near Jones, was dedicated July 29, 1877; corner stone was laid by the Masonic Grand Lodge, Oct. 13, 1875.

Bar Association of San Francisco was organized April 20, 1872.

"Barkeepers, Lives of Eminent;" by Jerry Thomas, S. F., 1863; "Alta" devoted nearly a column to the book, Nov. 10, 1863; see telegram in Sacramento Bee same date.

Barkan, Adolph; eminent oculist and aurist; has been established in S. F. since 1870; registered July 23, 1896, as born in Hungary, aged 52.

Barker, W. H., one of the original "San Francisco Minstrels," died Dec. 10, 1863.

Barnard, Archibald; was born in Montreal, Canada, Nov. 10, 1860; educated at St. Mary's College, and McGill University, Montreal, where he was admitted to the bar July 12, 1882; located in S. F. in Sept., 1889.

Barnes, Alexander, one of the original proprietors Cosmopolitan Hotel, died of general decline, Feb. 16, 1865.

Barnes, Geo. Ed., dramatic critic; one of the four practical printers who founded the "Call;" disposed of his interest in that paper in 1870; has since been dramatic editor for that and other city dailies; the while contributing weekly sketches of notable persons to the Call and Bulletin. Corrected in Supplement. See "Call."

Barnes, Wm. H.; Grand Scribe of the Grand Encampment of Odd Fellows; fraternal Society journalist; widely known as a leading spirit in fraternal orders and as a temperance and humorous speaker, since his advent in S. F. in 1878; was editor of the Weekly Call, 1879-86; fraternal society editor of the Examiner, 1887-88; registered Aug. 5, 1896, as born in Mass., aged 62. Prominent member of the First Baptist Church.

Barnes, Gen. William H. L.; distinguished lawyer and orator, was born at West Point, N. Y., Feb. 11, 1836; was educated at Yale College, in the class of 1855; studied law in Springfield, Mass.; before completing his legal studies, removed to N. Y. City, where he entered the office of Chas. O'Conor as managing Clerk, continuing his studies, while he retained that position, for four years. The war of the Rebellion breaking out, he entered the service, and was on

Gen. Fitz John Porter's staff. Contracting sickness in the field, he left the service and came to California, locating in S. F in April, 1863; Eugene Casserly invited him to a business connection, which was accepted. This association lasted until Mr. Casserly entered the U. S. Senate, in March, 1869; his appearance for the defendant in the great Sharon divorce case, gave him perhaps his widest celebrity. Was a member Second Constitutional Convention, 1878-79. He was long identified with the militia, being Colonel of the First Regiment for six years, and afterwards Major General, whence his title of "General," by which he is universally known. A chapter, of decided interest, is devoted to the General, in *Bench and Bar in California*.

Barnes, Wm. S.; who has been District Attorney since Jan., 1891, is the son of Gen. W. H. L. Barnes; he was born in S. F. in 1864, graduated from Harvard in 1886, prepared for the bar in Columbia Law College, and was admitted to practice in 1887; was united in marriage with a daughter of the bar leader, D. M. Delmas, in 1893.

Barnum, P. T.; famous showman; lectured on "The Art of Money Making," May 20, 1870.

Barrett & Sherwood, jewelers and chronometer makers, began business Dec., 1849; established the "City Observatory" on Telegraph Hill, 1850.

Barron, Wm. E.; wealthy citizen, of Bolton, Barron & Co., agents New Almaden Quicksilver Mines, died Oct. 25, 1871, aged 49.

Barrows, Rev. Chas. Dana, being called from Lowell, Mass., preached his first sermon as pastor of the First Congregational Church, May 22, 1881.

Barry, James H.; proprietor of "The Star," weekly newspaper, first issue of which was July 5, 1884; the article which caused his memorable commitment for contempt of Court, appeared in the Star of Aug. 3, 1889; arrested Oct. 1st, and released next day on bond of $500, by order of the Supreme Court; on Sunday, Oct. 5th, he addressed a Single Tax Meeting, on "Have We a Free Press?" The Act of the legislature, occasioned by his arrest, changing the law and procedure in contempt cases was introduced by Hon. Geo. Wentworth of S. F.; passed the Assembly Jan. 21, 1891, by a vote of 69 to 5, and the Senate, Feb. 4, by 32 to 6; signed by the Governor Feb. 17, 1891, and took immediate effect. It declared that no speech or publication should be treated as a contempt, unless made in the presence of the Court. Mr. Barry registered Aug. 1, 1896, as born in N. Y., aged 40.

Barry, Joseph E.; Justice of the Peace, three terms, 1893-98; registered July 23, 1896, as born in California, aged 28.

Barry, Theodore A., of noted retail liquor firm of Barry & Patten, died Aug. 27, 1881; native of Boston, Mass., aged 56.

Barstow, Dr. W. A.; a young physician in good practice, of fine appearance and popular ways, shot himself in the head, June 25th, and died July 20, 1870. He had very recently married Miss Eunice Rogers, singer and actress, daughter of another physician, Dr. Rogers, Quarantine Officer. A similar case was that of the English trage-dian, Walter Montgomery, who killed himself in London, in 1873, just after marriage. He had played in S. F. in 1870 – was here when Dr. Barstow committed suicide.

Bartlett, Columbus; prominent lawyer; was born in Columbus, Ga., Aug. 13, 1833; located in S. F. in Nov., 1852; admitted to the bar of the State Supreme Court in 1864; was deputy County Clerk under his brother Washington, July 1861 to July 1863; practiced law in part-nership with his brother (W. & C. Bartlett), 1866-70; in partner-ship with Leonidas E. Pratt (B. & P.), 1870-77; ran, as a Republican, for Superior Judge in 1882, his brother being, the same time, elected Mayor by the Democrats; Regent of the State University, vice Wm. Ashburner, deceased — term expiring in 1896.

Bartlett, Washington; sixteenth Governor of California; a pioneer of Nov. 13, 1849; printer and journalist; County Clerk three terms, 1859-63; 1868-69; State Senator, 1873-76; member Board of Freeholders to frame a City Charter, 1880; Mayor, and President Election Com-missioners and Board of Health, two terms, 1883-86; elected Gov-ernor of the State as a Democrat, Nov. 2, 1886; was inaugurated Jan. 8, 1887; died (the only California Governor who has died in office) at Oakland, Sept. 12, 1887; born in Georgia, Feb. 29, 1824.

Bartlett, Washington A.; first Alcalde of S. F. under American rule, 1846-47; gave the name of "San Francisco" to the settlement (before called Yerba Buena), Jan. 30, 1847.

Bartnett, Walter J.; was born at Pacheco, Contra Costa Co., Cal., May 22, 1866; attended the Boys High School, S. F., the University of California (College of Letters), receiving the degree of A. B., and Hastings College of the Law, from which he has the degree of LL. B.; admitted to the bar of the State Supreme Court, June, 1890; member of law firm of Gunnison, Booth & Bartnett since 1895.

Base Ball; the famous Red Stocking Club of Cincinnati, arrived overland, Sept. 22, 1869.

Baseball championship was won by the Athletics, Nov. 10, 1878.

Bassett, J. M.; veteran journalist; was a reporter on the S. F. Herald in 1870; editor Evening Post, 1873; of J. M. Bassett & Co., proprietors of The Portico, 1878; purchased the Golden Era in 1879, and sold it to Wagner & Bunyan in 1881; in 1882-83 was with the Wine and Tobacco Journal; editor of the American Standard, 1889; secretary of the American Standard Co., 1889-91; changed his residence to Oakland in 1884.

Bateman, Isaac E; prominent mining man; estate appraised at $113,166, Dec. 30, 1879.

Bates, Joseph C.; prominent lawyer; was born in Maine, July 1, 1836; grad-uate of Bowdoin College; located in S. F. April 30, 1866; admitted to the bar of the State Supreme Court the following year. Me-chanics' liens and street assessments have been his specialties.

Bay Sugar Refinery was established by Claus Spreckels in 1864; Mr.
   Spreckels sold it in 1866; it was leased to the S. F. and Pacific
   Sugar Refinery in 1867; the buildings were destroyed by fire,
   June 19, 1876. See " American Sugar Refinery."

Beachy, Hill; pioneer, and notable as an early stage line proprietor, died of
   paralysis, May 23, 1875; registered as a voter, Aug. 8, 1871, as a
   native of Penn., aged 43.

Beale, Edward F.; pioneer of July 15, 1846; U. S. Surveyor General for
   California, under President Lincoln; U. S. Minister to Austria, under President Grant; died in Washington, D. C., where he had
   long made his home, April 22, 1893; became a millionaire by
   speculations in California lands, and Washington City real estate.

Beard, E. L.; pioneer of May 28, 1849; died at Mission San Jose, May 8,
   1880; born in New York in 1818. Editorial notice in Bulletin, May
   11, 1880.

Beckwith, E. G.; Congregational clergyman; a moving speaker; author,
   among other papers, of " Ways that Have no Scriptural Warrant "
   — Oct. 5, 1885; removed, in 1887, to Honolulu, H. I., where, according to Rev. J. Q. Adams (Presbyterian) he established a church
   (the Central Union) which became " the great center of religious
   power in the kingdom."

Beecher, Henry Ward; delivered his first lecture in S. F., Aug. 22, 1878;
   preached to an immense congregation in the Grand Opera House,
   Sept. 1, 1878.

Beers, Geo. W.; well-known physician, unbalanced by bad fortune, murdered, with an iron bar, his wife, aged 28, and his daughter, aged
   9, and then killed himself by taking poison and severing an artery,
   at Mrs. Berry's lodging house, corner Stockton and Geary streets,
   July 2, 1863.

Beerstecher, Chas. J., member Second Constitutional Convention, 1878-79;
   was then aged 28; a native of Germany; Railroad Commissioner,
   1880-82.

Bees, Four colonies of, were shipped for New Zealand on steamship Australia, Nov. 20, 1880, being from the apiary of N. Levering, Los
   Angeles; each colony had an Italian " Queen."

Behre, Robert L.; a lawyer who was rapidly attaining distinction in his
   profession, died Sept, 10, 1885, native of N. Y., aged 32; was Assistant City and County Attorney in 1882.

Beideman, Jacob C.; the great landlord of the Western Addition; Assistant
   Alderman, July 1855 to July 1856; died July 8, 1865, leaving a very
   valuable estate in realty. Beideman & Page offered the State four
   blocks of land—bounded Van Ness, Gough, Eddy and O'Farrell
   streets—for a State Capitol site, Feb. 6, 1860.

Belcher, Edward A.; Judge of the Superior Court, by appointment, Oct. 25,
   1893, to fill a vacancy, and elected in Nov., 1894 for a term of six
   years from January, 1895; was born in Vt., Aug. 1, 1855; came to
   California and settled in Marysville in 1868; qualified himself for
   the bar in the office of his brothers, Isaac S. and Wm. C. Belcher

. at that place; was admitted to the bar of the Supreme Court Oct. 10, 1876; was elected City Attorney of Marysville the following year; lieut-col. on the staff of Governor Perkins, 1880-82; removed to S. F. in July, 1890.

Belcher, Isaac S.; distinguished jurist; was born in Vt., Feb. 27, 1825; graduated from the University of Vt., in 1846, admitted to the bar of the Supreme Court of that State in 1852; arrived in S. F., June 16, 1853; was District Attorney for Yuba County, 1856-57; District Judge of that district, 1864-69; Supreme Judge, March 4, 1872—Dec. 31, 1873; Member of the Constitutional Convention, 1878-79; one of the original trustees of the Stanford University; Supreme Court Commissioner since March 16, 1885.

Belknap, David P.; prominent lawyer; was born in N. Y. City in 1825; graduated from the University of N. Y. in 1844, admitted to the bar of the Supreme Court of that State; came to California in 1850, settling in San Jose; removed to S. F., 1852; from Oct., 1857 to 1859, was a deputy County Clerk. During this period he published his very useful book, "Belknap's Probate Practice," and also Bancroft's first Law and Form Book.

Bell, Alexander D., veteran journalist; while correspondent of the Post, was by the State Senate expelled from his desk in that Chamber, Jan. 10, 1874, for publishing a report that Senator Selden J. Finney had been bribed. On Jan. 13th the Senate revoked its action and appointed an investigating committee. On Jan. 20 the committee reported that Bell had only published a floating rumor, without malice; that although his act was injudicious, his expulsion had been too hasty, and a reconsideration of the Senate's action would be prudent. This recommendation was adopted with but one dissenting vote, that of Senator Finney himself. B. was secretary of the Gas Company in 1871, and registered as a voter Sept. 4, 1871, as a native of England, aged 45.

Bell, Gerrit W., assayer; Supervisor for the 8th Ward, 1862-66; was killed during his 3rd term by the great nitro-glycerine explosion in Wells, Fargo & Co's office, April 16, 1866. His home was at the corner of Pine and Leavenworth streets which later became the site of the elegant and commodious residence of Col. Chas. F. Crocker.

Bells; S. F. Brass and Bell Foundry, founded by W. T. Garratt, S. J. Derby, and W. H. Moore (W. T. G. & Co.), Dec., 1850; in 1855 the firm was Reed & Garratt (Geo. R. Reed). See Garratt, W. T.

"Bench and Bar in California;" imperial octavo volume, 550 pages—being a collection of delightful reminiscences and anecdotes of California Bar leaders—by Oscar T. Shuck—appeared, 1888.

Bench Show opened at Mechanics' Pavilion Oct. 29, 1877; 700 entries.

Benham, Calhoun; pioneer of Aug., 1849; Dis't Att'y, 1850; registered as a voter Sept. 1, 1868, as a native of Ohio, aged 44. See Fairfax.

Bennett, Nathaniel; one of the three Justices of the Supreme Court, elected by the legislature, Dec. 22, 1849; resigned, Oct. 3, 1851; died

April 20, 1886, native of N. Y., aged 68; estate appraised at $39,585;
Mrs. Bennett died Dec. 14, 1885, in her 50th year.

Beusley, John; pioneer of June 4, 1849; real estate broker; acquired large
means, and after extensive travels, died in the East, in 1889; his
widow died at Hot Springs, N. M., Dec. 30, 1889.   Sketch of Mr. B.,
by O. T. S., in Bulletin, Feb. 6, 1888; and of Mrs. B., same paper,
Jan. 9, 1890.

Benson, Sewall; real estate dealer, highly respected citizen, committed
suicide in Laurel Hill Cemetery, Oct. 7, 1868; a pioneer of Oct.
12, 1849.

Benton, John S.; one of the officers lost with the Brother Jonathan, and
Chas. H. Belden, U. S. Paymaster's Clerk, a victim of the same
disaster, were buried at S. F. Oct. 29, 1865.

Bergin & Sons, soap and candle makers, established, 1849.   Thomas Bergin
Sr., Thomas Bergin Jr., James, John and Michael Bergin.

Bergin, Thomas I., prominent lawyer, registered as a voter June 4, 1866, as
a native of Ireland, aged 30, and naturalized in U. S. District Court
at S. F., Aug. 1, 1859; member of the Board of Freeholders which
framed the proposed Charter of 1880.

Bergin, Michael; lawyer; brother of Thos. I.; died in the German Hospital, Aug. 3, 1893, leaving an estate of $5,000 cash, and several small
dwellings yielding good rents.

Berlin, Frederick Augustus, prominent lawyer; was born in Virginia, (now
West Virginia), Aug. 1, 1848; received his education in his native
State—at Roanoake College, Washington and Lee University, and
the University of Virginia; pursued legal study and took the de-
gree of Bachelor of Law at the last named institution; located in
S. F. in Feb., 1875.

Bermingham, John; President of the Cal'a Powder Works and Hercules
Powder Works since 1890, was Sup't of the Oregon & California
S. S. Co., 1865-68; with John Rosenfeld in the coal business, 1869-
71; shipping merchant, 1872-76; agent for steamship lines, 1877-
89; he was a School Director, 1878-79; registered as a voter July 9,
1866, as a native of N. Y., aged 37.

Bernal, Louis, after being convicted by a jury of murder in the first degree, which at that day left the Court no alternative to the death
penalty, was yet recommended by the jury to the mercy of the
Court, Aug. 11, 1850.   The death sentence was imposed, but a new
trial was granted, and the accused was acquitted, Sept. 10, 1850.

Berry, Campbell P., born in Alabama, Nov. 7, 1834; arrived in California,
1857; in Assembly from Sutter County, 1869-70; 1875-76; and
Speaker in 1877-78; member of Congress two terms, March 4, 1879
—March 4, 1883; U. S. Treasurer at S. F. under President Cleveland, 1893-97.

Berry, Gideon, M.; defaulting bookkeeper of Sheriff Matthew Nunan, and
defaulting secretary of the Mutual Building and Loan Society,
fled from the City Dec. 22, 1879.

Bert, Eugene Forster, born in S. F., of American parents, Feb. 13, 1866;

AMBROSE BEIRCE.

graduated from Hastings Law College in June, 1887, was admitted to the bar of the State Supreme Court in that year, and after June 1, 1891, was associated in practice with Hon. J. N. E. Wilson. At the 29th session of the legislature, 1891, he was a member of the Assembly; State Senator, 1895-97.

Berton, Francis; Consul of Switzerland and Portugal, Commander of the Order of Christ, died April 1, 1885; he had been cashier for many years of Henry Hentsch, his predecessor as banker and Consul; was born in Geneva, Switzerland, Feb. 4, 1830; Masonic burial; left a daughter in France. Mr. B. was a California pioneer of Nov. 21, '49.

Beveridge, Horatio, departed for Liverpool, England, March 31, 1883, intending to remain there as representative of Lund & Co., S. F.; had long been manager of the wool dep't of Falkner, Bell & Co.; returned after a few years and entered service of H. M. Newhall & Co.; resigned, and became manager of the "Pacific Coast Mining Agency," upon its organization in Jan., 1897.

Bianchi, Eugenio; popular, old time operatic tenor; came to S. F. from Mexico in 1857; died June 22, 1895, aged 72. Madame Bianchi died in Feb., 1895.

Bianchi, Eugenio, Jr.;son of the preceding, was born March 14, 1865, in S. F.; educated at the public Grammar and High Schools; pursued his law studies in the offices of Ferral & Payson, and A. D. Splivalo, and was admitted to the bar, Feb. 3, 1892.

Bierce, Ambrose; was Poet of the Day, July 4, 1889.

Bierstadt, Albert, renowned painter, arrived April 2, 1870; again, July 20, 1871.

Billiards; match between Joseph Little and Daniel Lynch, won by Little, July, 12, 1862.

Match between Wm. Goldthwaite and Harry Eaton, won by the former, Nov. 22, 1863.

Championship game between Cyrille Dion and John Deery, was won by Deery Jan. 8, 1870.

Dion beat Deery 181 points in 1000 on a carom table, Jan, 15, 1870.

Dion defeated Deery, Jan. 20, 1870.

Deery defeated Dion, Feb. 3, 1870.

Great champion match between John Deery and A. P. Rudolphe, was won by Rudolphe March 15, 1870.

Match between Deery and Rudolphe for charitable purposes, was won by Deery, March 18, 1870.

Pacific Coast Billiard Congress was organized May 4, 1870.

Pacific Coast Billard Tournament terminated May 17, 1870; the silver cue being awarded to J. W. Little.

Match for championship Pacific Coast between J. W. Little and J. F. B. McCleery, was won by Little, June 18, 1870.

Little defeated McCleery, Oct. 14, 1870.

Joseph Dion, distinguished billiardist, brother of Cyrille, arrived Nov. 4, 1870.

McCleery defeated Little for the silver cue and the championship of California, Nov. 18, 1870.

Match between Joseph Dion and John Deery was won by Dion,
Nov. 26, 1870.

Same players contested for $1000, Jan. 12, 1871, Dion winning.

Same players, for $500 a side, Jan. 26, 1871, Deery winning.

Same, for same, Feb. 9, 1871, Deery winning.

Match between Joseph Dion and A. P. Rudolphe, for $1000 a
side, March 15, 1871, won by Dion.

A. P. Rudolphe and Joseph Dion, April 1, 1871, $1000 a side,
won by Rudolphe.

Cyrille Dion and John Deery, for $1000 a side, April 7, 1871,
won by Dion.

Cyrille Dion and Joseph Dion, played against John Deery and
A. P. Rudolphe for $500 a side, April 8, 1871, the brothers winning.

Joseph Dion and A. P. Rudolphe, for $1000 a side, April 17,
1871, Dion winning.

J. F. B. McCleery and J. H. Mott, Jr., Sept. 9, 1871, McCleery
winning.

McCleery defeated Waite by 500 points, March 21, 1872.

Match between McCleery and Kraker, was won by the latter,
May 7, 1872.

Match between Lance Perkins and Henry Merryfield for $500
a side, was won by Perkins, June 10, 1873.

The Billiard Tournament for the championship of the Pacific
Coast, resulted in the first prize, a silver cue, being awarded to J.
F. B. McCleery, Aug. 30, 1873.

Match between Anthony Kraker and John F. B. McCleery,
for the championship of the Pacific Coast and the silver cue, was
won by Kraker, Oct. 25, 1873.

Anthony Kraker defeated John Deery in a match for $1,000, Aug.
14, 1875.

Grand Tournament began at Platt's Hall, the players being
Albert Gardiner, William Sexton, Maurice Daly and Geo. L.
Slosson, July 31, 1876.

Billings, Frederick; pioneer of April 1, 1849; prominent and wealthy
lawyer; died at the age of 67, at Woodstock, Vt., his native State,
whither he had returned some twenty years before, on Sept. 30,
1890. For his first "start," see "Getting a Start in the World,"
in S. F. Bulletin, Sept. 5, 1885.

B'nai B'rith, Independent Order of, laid the corner stone of their new hall
on Eddy street, Sept. 22, 1878.

B'nai B'rith, Order of ; Hall dedicated July 13, 1879.

Bingham, Henry; Supervisor, 1889-90; author of the Bingham Ordinance,
passed by the Supervisors in 1890, providing for confining the
Chinese population of the City within certain prescribed limits;
declared unconstitutional, Aug. 25, 1890.

Bingham, James W.; License Collector, jointly with N. Proctor Smith,

1860-61; Clerk of Board of Supervisors, 1861-68; died in that office, of consumption, April 26, 1868, aged 47; native of N. Y.

Birds passed over the western part of the city in such numbers, as to darken the sky, Jan. 31, 1871.

Birdsall, Dr. L. A.; pioneer of June 27, 1849; Superintendent of the Mint under President Pierce; died in Oakland, March 1, 1886, a native of N. Y., aged 84. He was father of Milton S. Latham's first wife, Sophie, in whose memory the figure of Hope, in Italian marble, is a beautiful and striking object in Laurel Hill Cemetery; left a large estate.

Bisbee, ex-Judge D. W. F.; died May 8, 1885; native of N. Y., aged 65 years, 9 months.

Bishop, Thomas B.; prominent lawyer; Member Board of Freeholders to frame a City Charter, 1880; registered as a voter, June 5, 1866, as a native of Mass., aged 25.

Bixler, David; distinguished lawyer; practiced in S. F. some ten years, part of the time in association, but not in partnership, with Eugene Casserly, then removed to Virginia City, Nev., in 1865; there, in partnership with Gen. Thos. H. Williams, he amassed a great fortune at the bar and in mining ventures; returned to S. F. in 1879; registered July 30, 1896, as born in Maryland, aged 65.

Black, Alfred Pressly; was born in Pa., Nov. 26, 1856; located in S. F. Oct., 1882; was prepared for the bar in Hastings College, graduated with the class of '85; he has been Assistant District Attorney under Hon. Wm. S. Barnes, since 1891.

Black Bass, a monster specimen of, caught in the bay, Oct. 13, 1859; length 7 feet 1 inch; weight 300 pounds.

Black, Mary; first woman pioneer of California, died Sept. 17, 1876.

Black Will Case, fourth trial of; resulted in a verdict that the testator was not of sound mind, April 2. 1874.

Blackburn, William; pioneer of Sept. 23, 1845; Judge of First Instance at Santa Cruz under U. S. Military government before State organization; died at S. F. March 24, 1867, aged 58.

Blake, Chas. E., Sr.; prominent dentist; pioneer of Sept., 1849; has followed his profession in S. F. from that date; inventor of several important dental instruments; was born in Mass., in 1823.

Blake, James; distinguished physician of S. F.; died at Middletown, Lake Co., Cal., June, 1893; native of England, aged 78.

Blake, M. C.; Assemblyman in 1857, County Judge, 1857-63; Probate Judge, 1864-67; Judge Municipal Criminal Court, 1879; Mayor, and President of Election Commissioners, New City Hall Commissioners, and Board of Health, 1882 (one year); decided, as Probate Judge, in favor of the validity of the alleged will of Dav. C. Broderick, Otc. 8, 1860.

Blake, Maurice B.; nephew of the last named, was born in Me., Jan. 6, 1845; graduated from Amherst College in 1866; located in S. F. in the Spring of 1868; admitted to the bar of the State Supreme Court, April 5, 1870; died Feb. 8, 1886.

Blanding, Gordon; son of the next named; prominent lawyer; registered in 1896, as born in S. C., aged 46.

Blanding, William; U. S. District Attorney under President Pierce, appointed July 15, 1856; State Harbor Commissioner by appointment of Gov. Irwin, March, 1876 to March, 1882. A sketch of his life is in Bancroft's Contemporary Biography.

Blitz, B. S., noted police officer since 1852, died at Warm Springs, Alameda Co., July 13, 1868; native of Holland, aged 42.

Block, James N.; Tax Collector and Election Commissioner for three terms, 1893-98; registered June 13, 1896, as born in Miss., aged 56.

Blossom Rock, near Alcatraz Island was destroyed (under a contract with the federal government) by A. W. Von Schmidt, by a submarine blast, April 23, 1870; a beautiful spectacle witnessed by many thousands of people, gathered principally on Telegraph hill; Col. Von Schmidt received under his contract $75,000, Dec. 8, 1870.

Boalt, John H.; distinguished lawyer; a native of Ohio, born March 29, 1837; graduate of Amherst College; qualified as a mining and mechanical Engineer at Heidelberg and Freiberg; was a lieutenant in the war of the Rebellion; amassed a fortune in Nevada as one of the Stetefeldt Furnace Co., owning a new process for reducing ores; District Judge for Lander Co., Nev., term ending in 1871; located in S. F. in that year. (Sketch in Bench and Bar.) An article by him, on "The Silver Question," is in the Overland Monthly, Nov. 1, 1886.

Board of Trade was organized April, 1877.

Boat Race between the Pioneer and South End Rowing Clubs, for $550, was won by the first named March 17, 1874.

Board of Brokers. On June 12, 1875, there were 9 vacant seats, for which there were 20 applicants ready to pay $25,000 each; a seat sold for $30,000, Jan. 21, 1875.

Bohemian Club was incorporated May 17, 1872.

Bohen, Geo. T.; Superintendent of Streets two terms, 1861-64; Fire Commissioner since Oct. 3, 1893; President of the Board 1896-97; registered as a voter June 2, 1866, as a native of Maryland, aged 43.

Bolton, Barron & Co., commission merchants, and agents New Almaden Quicksilver Mine, organized 1850; James R. Bolton, Wm. E. Barron.

Bolton & Barron Land Claim, affecting a large portion of the landed area of S. F., confirmed by the U. S. Land Commission, June 5, 1855.

Bolton, James R., wealthy citizen, of Bolton, Barron & Co., Agents New Almaden Quicksilver Mine, died Jan. 28, 1890, native of N. Y., aged 73.

Bonanza Suit of John H. Burke vs. James C. Flood et al.; decision of Superior Judge J. F. Sullivan in favor of plaintiff for 6125 shares of Consolidated Virginia Mining Co.'s stock and 3573 shares California Mining Co.'s stock, March 30,1881.

Bonner, Charles; Superintendent, at Virginia City, Nev., of the Gould & Curry Mine, in the middle Sixties, died at S. F., Aug. 31, 1871, leaving a snug fortune to his widow and three children.

Bonner, John; veteran editor, literary critic and reviewer; editor Chronicle, 1885-86; editor Call, 1887-91; editorial writer, 1892-94; editor Bulletin, 1895-97; lectured at Stanford University, Feb. 17, 1897, under auspices of the Stanford Press Club, on his work in journalism, and the historic personages with whom he had been familiar.

Bonnet, Jennie; an interesting French girl, known, from her vocation ,as the "Frog Catcher," was assassinated Sept. 15, 1876.

Bookbinders' Protective and Beneficial Association of S. F., Local Union No. 31 was organized Aug. 15, 1875.

Booker, Wm. Lane, for many years H. B. M. Consul at S. F., was on the eve of his departure for N. Y. City to become H. B. M. Consul-General for the U. S., presented by the Board of Fire Underwriters and leading merchants with a model of a Sierra redwood tree, of pure silver, oxydized, March 26, 1883.

Boone, John L.; was born in Iowa, Aug. 5, 1843; entered the Wesleyan University at Delaware, Ohio, from which he withdrew in Aug., 1861, to enlist in the war of the Rebellion; was discharged in Nov., 1862. In 1866 was clerk of the lower house of the Oregon legislature; in 1867 removed to S. F. and formed a connection with Dewey & Co., publishers and patent solicitors, whose patent agency he managed for eleven years. In July, 1877, was admitted to the bar of our Supreme Court; since then has made patent law a specialty; State Senator, 26th session, 1885.

Booth, Adam; a prominent produce commission merchant, died Oct. 30 1876; registered as a voter Sept. 30, 1868, as a native of Penn., aged 54.

Booth, A. G.; prominent lawyer; Assemblyman, leading the Republican minority, 1884; member of Board of Freeholders which framed the defeated City Charter of 1886; was born in N. H. in 1845; admitted to the bar in 1870.

Booth, Newton; presided at citizens' meeting to protest against Congress ceding Goat Island to the C. P. R. R. Co., Jan. 4, 1873. While Governor of the State, lectured in Pacific Hall on *Charles James Fox*, Feb. 24, 1875; a finely written notice from his pen, of the great but eccentric S. F. lawyer, Lockwood, is in the "Overland Monthly," 1870; copied by the Albany, N. Y., Law Journal.

Bootz Hotel, corner Pine street and Belden Place (20x57½), was sold by Adam Bootz to Pierre Priet and wife for $27,000, Oct. 24, 1881. Mr. Bootz, who had kept the Philadelphia House, and later the Sacramento Hotel, and the New York Hotel, opened the Bootz Hotel in 1861, and conducted it to its sale in 1881, and for two years later; he then opened Bootz Park, on the Mission Road, which he maintained to 1895; Adam J. Bootz, proprietor, 1896-97.

Boston Excursion Party arrived June 1, 1870.

Botts, Charles T.; prominent lawyer, and pioneer, distinguished member of the first Constitutional Convention, 1849; defeated by E. J. C. Kewen for Attorney General by one vote in the legislature, Dec.

22, 1849; registered as a voter July 5, 1866, as a native of Virginia, aged 57. See Supplement.

Bourn, Wm. B.; was established as a commission merchant in June, 1850; died July 24, 1874, leaving a large estate; a native of Mass., aged 64.

Bourn, Wm. B.; manager of Wm. B. Bourn's estate; was elected Nov. 6, 1894, a member of the Board of Freeholders which framed the proposed City Charter that was defeated at the general election of Nov. 3, 1896; but the Supreme Court adjudged him to be ineligible because not a qualified elector of the City for five years prior to his election; registered July 31, 1896, as born in California, aged 39.

Bowie, Augustus J.; veteran physician and surgeon; was born in Maryland, Oct. 23, 1815; died at S. F. July 6, 1887; funeral rites of the Catholic Church.

Bowers, Geo. W.; millionaire mining man of S. F., died in June, 1893.

Bowman, James F., poet and journalist, died April 29, 1882, native of Columbia Co., N. Y., aged 56; funeral from Trinity Episcopal Church.

Boyd, Colin M.; Auditor, Election Commissioner, and New City Hall Commissioner, May-Nov., 1879; Supervisor, two terms, 1887-90; member of the Board of Freeholders, which framed the proposed City Charter, defeated at the general election, Nov. 3, 1896; Fire Commissioner since 1895; registered as a voter July 29, 1867, as a native of Scotland, aged 36.

Boyd, James T.; prominent and wealthy lawyer, registered as a voter, June 1, 1866, as a native of N. Y., aged 40; member of the Board of Freeholders which framed the defeated City Charter of 1880.

Boys and Girls Aid Society was incorporated Sept. 15, 1874; first annual meeting was held, and permanent organization effected, June 2, 1874.

Brady, Matthew; Second Assistant Engineer Fire Department, Sept. 19, 1870 to April 6, 1874; First Assistant Engineer, April 6, 1874-81; Assistant Chief Engineer, 1881 to Sept. 21, 1882, on which day he was killed by accident while on duty.

Bragg, Geo. F.; prominent shipping and commission merchant for thirty years, died July 18, 1879; native of N. Y., aged 68; one of the founders of the Pacific Woolen Mills, and for many years President of the first R. R. Co. in the State (Sacramento Valley R. R.).

Bradford, A. C.; pioneer of July 5, 1849; early County Judge, San Joaquin Co.; member of Assembly, 1854; defeated Democratic candidate for Police Judge, S. F., 1877; Assistant District Attorney, S. F., under Hon. Wm. Craig, 1883; Register U. S. Land office under President Cleveland, 1886; accidentally killed by a street car in 1889.

Brandon, Frederick D.; born at Cambridge, England, April 30, 1846; located in S. F. May, 1876; admitted to the bar of the State Supreme Court, in July, 1880.

Brandon, Joseph R.; well-known lawyer; was the cause of a change in the law of this State, concerning the admission of persons to practice law. The original Act of Feb. 19, 1851; permitted only the admission of citizens. Mr. B. not having become a citizen, applied to the legislature in 1860, to pass a law authorizing the Courts to admit him to the bar, after examination. Senator Solomon A. Sharp introduced the bill, which was amended at the instance of the Senate judiciary committee by adding the proviso that Mr. B. should first declare his intention to become a citizen. The bill did not pass, but at the next session a general law was adopted, amending that of 1851, so as to allow the admission to the bar, not only of citizens, but those who had declared their intention to become such. Mr. B. was born in Barbadoes, where his father was an English sugar planter, Jan. 8, 1828. He was educated in England, and admitted to the bar in S. F.

Brannan Samuel; arrived in California per ship Brooklyn, July 31, 1846; issued the California Star, Jan., 1847, first newspaper in S. F.; opened a general store at Sutter's Fort (Sacramento), in fall of '47; was a member of the Town Council, Aug. 6, 1849-May 8, 1850. He acquired and lost a very large estate; among his money transactions was a loan of $430,478 to the Government of Mexico, Sept., 1865, for 60 days. He died at Escondido, San Diego Co., and was buried in the San Diego Cemetery. See Supplement.

Breeze, Thomas; a partner in 1859 of Eugene Kelly, Daniel T. Murphy, Joseph A. Donohoe and Adam Grant (Eugene Kelly & Co.), importers dry goods; in 1866-74, was of Murphy, Grant & Co.; died April 6, 1874, native of Ireland, aged 53.

Brenham, Chas. J.; pioneer of Aug. 18, 1849; Whig Mayor, May, 1851-Jan., 1852; and Nov., 1852-Oct., 1853; Park Commissioner, 1872; died May 10, 1875; native of Ky., aged 58.

Brewer, John H., born in Mass., in 1824; graduate of Yale College; admitted to the bar in his native county, 1853; located in S. F., June, 1854; a member of the Board of Education, 1859-60; has removed to Oakland.

Brewers' Protective Association was incorporated Sept. 14, 1874.

Bricklayers began work under the eight-hour rule, Feb. 1, 1867.

Bridge, Samuel J.; established the Bridge Medal Fund for Boys of the S. F. Grammar Schools, April 16, 1879; amount donated, $2,000; he was then residing in Dresden, Maine, but was visiting S. F.; he was then 70 years old, having been born in Boston, Mass., June 1, 1809. A notice of his life and of the Fund he established, is in Municipal Reports, 1878-79, pages 749-752. In S. F. from 1861 to 1869, Mr. B. was an appraiser in the Custom House, being Appraiser General the first two years. On Aug. 20, 1873, he presented to the State a portrait of Manuel Micheltorena, Mexican Governor of California, 1842-45. The correspondence is in Assembly Journal of 20th Session, pages 1128, 1129.

Brierley, Rev. Benjamin; pastor First Baptist Chruch, S. F., May, 1852 to May, 1858, died at Nevada City, July 21, 1863.

Briggs, Wm. R.; noted sporting man, pioneer of Aug. 8, 1849; registered as a voter June 5, 1866, as a native of Missouri, aged 35—a candi* man who once laid a wager that his native city, St. Louis, was the largest in the world, and who, on registering as a voter, put himself down as a gambler.

Bright and beautiful day closed the year 1866, after a long season of disastrous storms.

British Benevolent Society was incorporated in 1865.

British Mutual Benefit Association was organized May 10, 1876.

Britt, James E.; Assemblyman, 1887; State Senator, 1889-91; Supervisor, 1897-98.

Brittan, J. W.; Alderman, July, 1855—July, 1856; died in N. Y. City, April 8, 1872, aged 52.

Brittan, Wm. G.; lawyer, son of the preceding; Justice of the Peace, 1891-92; registered Aug. 5, 1896, as born in Switzerland, of American parents, aged 32.

Britton, Joseph; pioneer of Oct. 5, 1849; Supervisor, 1860-61; President of the Board of Freeholders which framed the proposed Charter, defeated at the general election, Nov. 3, 1896; registered June 9, 1896, as born in England, aged 71.

Broderick, David C.; pioneer of June 13, 1849; State Senator, 1st, 2nd and 3rd Sessions; President State Senate, 1851; U. S. Senator, March 4, 1857 to Sept. 16, 1859, when he died from a wound received in a duel with Supreme Judge David S. Terry near Lake Merced, S. F.; his alleged will, with John A. McGlynn and A. J. Butler as executors, was admitted to probate by Judge M. C. Blake, after a severe contest, Oct. 8, 1860. His estate was by order of the Court sold at public sale, by Cobb, Sinton & Bond, auctioneers, and realized $170,350.

Broderick Monument, in Lone Mountain Cemetery, work was begun on Sept. 24, 1862; corner stone laid by Gov. Stanford, Feb. 22, 1863.

Broderick, William; Assemblyman, 1875-76 and 1877-78; Auditor, Election Commissioner, and New City Hall Commissioner, three terms, 1893-98; registered as a voter July 27, 1871, as a native of Ireland, aged 39.

Brokers; S. F. Stock Board; the fine building on Pine street was occupied Oct. 1, 1877; corner stone laid, April 27, 1876.

Bromley, Geo. T.; popular lecturer and humorist; conductor on the first steam railway in the State (between Sacramento and Folsom), in the late Fifties; since street contractor in S. F.; Port Warden under Gov. Perkins for four years, from March 29, 1880; U. S. Consul at Tientsin, China, 1884-87; registered as a voter, Sept. 2, 1871, as a native of Connecticut, aged 53. Received an album from the Bohemian Club on his 75th birthday.

Bronze Statue, the first work of the kind accomplished on the Pacific Coast, was placed over the grave of Mrs. Wm. T. Garratt in Masonic Cemetery, Jan. 8, 1880; height 7½ feet; weight 1200 pounds; was cast at the foundry of Wm. T. Garratt.

Brooklyn Hotel, Bush street; was opened by Kelly & Wood, in 1867; Mr. Kelly had for many years kept hotel under the same name at other locations. The property belonged to Dr. C. M. Hitchcock; the brick building had been erected in 1854, and enlarged in Sept., 1867.

Brooks, Benjamin S., prominent lawyer, who, twenty years prior, owned the Ocean Side House and surrounding territory, died April 29, 1884; registered as a voter, June 8, 1866, as a native of Connecticut, aged 46; estate appraised Sept. 1, 1884, at $81,000 (nearly all land, in five counties).

Brooks, S. H.; State Controller, Jan., 1860 to Nov. 20, 1861, when he resigned; was field counsellor of Judge Terry in the duel with Broderick, Sept., 1859; stock broker, 1874 to 1886, when he became U. S. Treasurer at S. F., by appointment of President Cleveland, and served four years; registered Sept. 28, 1872, as born in Tenn., aged 41.

Brother Jonathan Steamship was lost near Crescent City, Cal., July, 1865; news received at S. F. Aug. 1, 1865.

Brotherton Brothers; forgers; second trial of, resulted in a verdict of guilty, Oct. 31, 1872; the brothers escaped from the County Jail, Nov. 3, 1872; they were recaptured Nov. 8, 1872.

Brown, Charles, who came to S. F. on a whaler, in 1829, died Feb. 15, 1883, native of N. Y., aged 68.

Brown, Harvey S.; pioneer of Oct. 16, 1849; District Attorney 1858-61; resigned July 2, 1861; land agent of the Central Pacific R. R., 1872-73; one of the Attorneys for the C. P. R. R., the S. P. R. R., and the Southern Pacific Company continuously since 1875; one of the Attorneys for the Williams claimants in the great Blythe case.

Brown, John; first American Justice of the Peace at S. F. See Cal. Supreme Court Reports, vol. I, page 583.

Brown, Wm. E.; Vice President in 1897 of Crocker-Woolworth National Bank, was Private Secretary of Gov. Stanford, 1862-63, and of Gov. Low, 1864-67; removed from Sacramento to S. F. in 1877; President of the Pacific Improvement Co., 1891-93; was a Director of the Southern Pacific Company, 1888-91; author of a sketch of Leland Stanford, in " Representative Men."

Bruner, Dr. Wm. H.; pioneer of Aug. 1, 1849; prominent physician, died Aug. 10, 1886, native of Penn., aged 60 years.

Bryan, Wm. J.; pioneer of Oct. 11, 1849; leading druggist; Recorder of Deeds, etc., 1883-84; Postmaster under President Cleveland for four years ending July 1, 1890; registered as a voter July 29, 1867, as a native of Scotland, aged 28.

Bryant, Andrew J.; Mayor, and President New City Hall Commissioners and Board of Health, two terms, 1876-79; drowned in S. F. Bay, May 11, 1888, native of New Hampshire, aged 53. The great anti-Chinese riots (see Chinese), occurred during his first term.

Bryant, Edwin; third Alcalde of S. F. under American rule, assumed office Feb. 22, 1847; author of " What I Saw in California;" Bryant street is named for him.

Buckingham, Aurelius A.; veteran pilot, was lost off the Golden Gate with the pilot boat Caleb Curtis, and two other pilots, Captains Van Ness and Schander, April 12, 1867.

Buckley, Dr. C. F.; the attempt to assassinate him by Sarah R. Yokum, occurred Oct. 1, 1874.

Buckley, John P.; pioneer of Sept. 7, 1849; State Senator, 1863-64; of Graves, Williams & Co. fruit and commission merchants; died Nov. 17, 1864, from injuries received (his ankle having caught in a coil of rope) at the launch of the U. S. iron-clad Comanche.

Buehler, Rev. J. M., of St. Paul German Evangelical Lutheran Church, began his long and fruitful pastorate of that Church in 1862. He is not foreign born, as generally understood, but registered as a voter Sept. 2, 1867, as a native of Maryland, aged 30.

Bugbee, John S., Assistant City and County Attorney under John Lord Love, 1885-86, fell dead at Juneau, Alaska, while presiding over a turbulent political convention, May 16, 1896; he was father of Maxwell G., Winslow, and Arthur Bugbee, and Mrs. L. H. Tarpley, and brother of Sumner W. Bugbee and Mrs. Ella H. Hughes; a native of New Brunswick, aged 56.

Bugbee, S. C.; prominent architect; Assemblyman, 1865-66; School Director, 1866-67; died Sept. 1, 1877, a native of New Brunswick, aged 65.

Buisley, Joseph G.; a famous aeronaut, died from a fall from a balloon, Oct. 13, 1874.

Bulkhead Bill of 1860; the S. F. Dock and Wharf Co., to which this famous bill, vetoed by Gov. Downey, proposed to practically give away the City water front, was composed of Dr. H. S. Gates, J. Mora Moss, John Nightingale, Abel Guy, John B. Felton, John Crane, and Levi Parsons; the bill was vetoed April 17, 1860; the Governor arriving from the Capital, was publicly received by a torchlight procession, pyrotechnic display, and salvos of artillery, May 1, 1860.

Bull, Alpheus; pioneer of July 27, 1849; an early day banker, (Bull, Baker & Co.); President Gould & Curry Mining Co., 1865-72; President Savage Mining Co., 1867-71; Vice-President Firemen's Fund Ins. Co., 1873-83 and 1890; was drowned at Fort Point, in presence of his wife, May 16, 1890, aged 76; a Quaker; native of N. Y.

Bull, Franklin P.; well-known lawyer, was born in Wisconsin in 1854; graduated from the public Schools of that State; was clerk and law student in the office of D. M. Delmas, in San Jose; admitted to the bar of the State Supreme Court in 1882, and of the U. S. Courts in 1885.

Bull Fight at the "Willows" July 14, 1859; the conductor thereof, Garcia Yanez, was tried and acquitted by a jury July 21st. For full description of another bull fight at the same place, see local press, Aug. 18, 1859.

Bulletin, Daily Evening; the first number was issued Oct. 8, 1855, by C. O. Gerberding & Co.; James King of Wm., editor; it began using an eight-cylinder Hoe press, Jan. 5, 1870. The paper was sold by

order of Court, to settle the partnership between Geo. K. Fitch
and the estates of Loring Pickering and James W. Simonton, Jan.
10, 1895, and was purchased by R. A. Crothers.

The Bulletin published the questions which had been prepared
in the State Superintendent's office for teachers' examination,
Nov. 28, 1878; much investigation and tribulation followed.

Bunker Hill Association was organized in 1860.

Bunker, Wm. M. purchased the Daily Report in 1875, and converted it
from a mining stock circular into a general newspaper. A. C,
Hiester became his partner in the paper in 1877; Mr. B. had been
City editor of the Bulletin, and was at the front, corresponding
with that journal, in the short but sanguinary Modoc war, 1873.
He is a native of Mass., born in 1850.

Burbank, Caleb; Member of Assembly, 1858; State Senator for 12th Session, 1861; resigned July 30; District Judge, Storey Co., Nevada,
1865-66. For his contest with Judge Hager for the office of District Judge S. F., see 12th vol. California Reports, page 378.

Burch, John C., State Senator for Trinity and Humboldt, 1858-59; Member
of Congress March 4, 1859-March 4, 1861; died at S. F. where he
had resided many years, Aug. 31, 1885, native of Missouri, aged
59; was Attorney for absent heirs in the estate of Thomas H.
Blythe, by appointment of Judge Coffey, at his death.

Burke, Ethelbert; pioneer of Sept. 20, 1849; Member of Assembly from
Mariposa, 1855; later District Judge of that district; Justice of the
Peace at S. F., in 1880, and again in 1885-88; Presiding Justice of
the Peace, 1885-86; registered as a voter, June 15, 1866, as a native
of Virginia, aged 46.

Burke, Martin J.; head of the long established house of Madison & Burke;
was chief of Police, 1858-65; registered as a voter June 13, 1866, as
a native of Ireland, aged 45. See Madison & Burke.

Burlingame, Anson, U. S. minister to China, and Col. Van Valkenburg,
U. S. Minister to Japan, were banqueted by the Chinese merchants, May 31, 1866.

Burnett, John M.; prominent lawyer; son of Peter H. Burnett; School Director, two terms, 1868-71, and President of the Board, 1870-71;
registered as a voter June 19, 1866, as a native of Missouri, aged 28.

Burnett, Peter H.; first Governor of the State of California, 1850; resigned
the office Jan. 9, 1851; a pioneer of Nov. 5, 1848; lawyer and banker; born in Tennessee, Nov. 15, 1807; died at S. F., in sleep, May
17, 1895; funeral from St. Ignatius Catholic Church.

Burnett, W, C.; prominent lawyer; State Senator for Yuba and Sutter,
1856-57; City and County Attorney of S. F., four terms, 1871-79;
New City Hall Commissioner and Election Commissioner, the
same period; registered as a voter May 23, 1866, as a native of
Conn., aged 37.

Burns, Daniel M.; widely known politician, and mining man; was appointed Police Commissioner, vice R. P. Hammond, deceased, Dec. 2,
1891, and continued in office to Jan. 5, 1895, when he resigned; was

the first Secretary of State under the present Constitution, holding for three years ending in Jan., 1883.

Burns, Henry J.; Captain of the Sumner Light Guard, won the first prize at the Shooting Tournament of the California Rifle Association, Oct. 25, 1875, the tournament opening Oct. 22d.

Burns, Robert; centennial anniversary of his birth was observed by a banquet at the Oriental Hotel, Jan. 25, 1859; George Gordon presided, and the eloquent E. D. Baker spoke to "The Press;" there was also what was said to be a banquet with more rollicking glee, at the Tremont House the same night.

Burr, E. W.; Mayor, Oct., 1857-Oct., 1859; first President of the first S. F. savings bank, The Savings and Loan Society, incorporated July 23, 1857; died July 21, 1894; a native of Rhode Island, aged 85.

Burrowes, Rev. Geo., D. D., Congregationalist, Professor of Greek and Hebrew in the Theological Seminary, S. F., completed his reading of the Greek Testament for the three hundred and twelfth time, Sept. 21, 1887.

Burton, Edward F.; Assemblyman, Nev. Co., 1854, being one of ten Whigs in a body of 80 members; State Senator, from same county, 1855-56; State Controller Feb. 25, April 21, 1857; Superintendent U. S. Mint at S. F., 1882 to July, 1885, appointed by President Arthur at request of Senator Sargent; a California pioneer of Aug. 29, 1849; died at Denver, Col., May 11, 1891.

Bush, David; a public spirited citizen, to whose bounty the well remembered "Bush Fund" (to furnish employment in the Park for needy laborers) owed its origin; so many citizens contributed to his fund, that on some days in February and March, 1880, he had to employ a man specially to receive their contributions. Mr. B. was a School Director in 1881.

Butchertown Controversy of 1879-80; the merits of the respective sides are set forth in opposing cards in the city press of Jan. 12, 1880—one signed by A. J. Donnelly, the other by Miller & Lux, Moses Selig, Wm. Dunphy, Poly & Co., M. Brandenstein and J. Schoenfeld.

Butterworth, Samuel F.; wealthy mining operator; regent of the State University; Park Commissioner, 1870-71; 1873-75; died May 5, 1875; registered as a voter July 22, 1867, as a native of N. Y., aged 55.

Byrne, Henry Herbert; distinguished lawyer; A native of N. Y. City, and came to S. F. at the age of 26; was District Attorney for four terms, 1851-52; 1853-54; 1868-69; 1870-71. In 1854 he married the celebrated actress, Matilda Heron, from whom he shortly separated. He died at S. F., March 1, 1872, aged 48, leaving an estate worth $90,000. Byrne's brilliant and romantic career is the subject of a chapter in "Bench and Bar in California." See "Heron, Matilda," and Carpentier, E. R.

Byrne, Lafayette; brother of the preceding, was thrown from a buggy, April 26th, and died from the injuries May 20, 1864.

Byrnes, J. D.; was Joint State Senator for San Francisco and San Mateo, residing in San Mateo, for five sessions; 1880-81; 1887-91.

C

Cable Railways. See Clay Street Railroad. As to the contention that Gen. P. G. T. Beauregard was (in 1870) the inventor of cable railways, see Bulletin, May 23, 1881, page 4; see also Hallidie, A. S.

Calderwood, David; whose life in S. F., was spent in litigation, died Nov. 7, 1882; native of Scotland, aged 65; for his suit against Supreme Judges Norton, Cope, and Crocker, see local press, Feb. 24, 1864.

Caledonian Club was organized Nov. 24, 1866; incorporated Aug. 26, 1871.

"California Anthology"—octavo vol., 471 pages—being gems of thought selected from California writers, by Oscar T. Shuck; Barry and Baird, publishers; appeared in 1880.

California Bible Society was organized, Oct. 30, 1849.

California Brewery was established in 1850.

California Chronicle; (not to be confounded with the S. F. Chronicle, established in 1868) daily newspaper, first appeared Nov. 21, 1853; Frank Soulé & Co., proprietors.

California Farmer; weekly newspaper; was established by Warren & Co., Jan. 1, 1864.

California Historical Society was incorporated April 19, 1852.

California Market was inaugurated, July 31, 1867; Lloyd Tevis and Albert E. Davis, owners.

California Olympic Club was organized Nov. 11, 1871.

California Pioneers, Society of; was organized Aug., 1850; incorporated, Jan. 28, 1863; Hall of, on Montgomery street, between Jackson and Pacific, was opened Jan. 8, 1863; Hall on Fourth street near Market was opened and occupied in 1886.

California Prison Commission was organized Nov. 27, 1865.

"California Rifles" N. G. C., were mustered out of service by order of Gov. Haight, Nov. 3, 1871.

California Safe Deposit and Trust Company was incorporated April 24, 1882; it had been styled, since its foundation in 1875, the Safe Deposit Company of S. F. Eugene Casserly was its first President. The institution was the "idea" of Joseph C. Duncan, its real founder, who invited Mr. Casserly to the Presidency, and selected Frank E. R. Whitney as Chief of Patrol.

"California Scrap Book"—octavo volume, 705 pages—a repository of select reading, compiled by Oscar T. Shuck, and published by H. H. Bancroft & Company, appeared in 1869.

California State Telegraph Co.; line was opened between S. F. and San José, Oct. 1, 1853.

California Steam Navigation Co., was organized March 1, 1854.

California Stock Exchange Board was organized Jan. 20, 1872.

California Street Railroad, work was begun July 15, 1877; was opened for traffic April 10, 1878.

California Sugar Refinery was established by Claus Spreckels in 1867, at Brannan and Elizabeth streets; the corner stone of the mammoth Refinery on the Potrero was laid, May 28, 1881; the plant, buildings and equipment cost $1,500,000; the Refinery was set in operation in Jan., 1883, with a capacity of 80,000 to 100,000 tons of refined sugar per annum, and employing 500 men.

California Theater; Bush street between Kearny and Dupont, was opened to the public Jan. 18, 1868.

Calkin, Milo; pioneer of June 4, 1849; died at San Rafael, April 25, 1872, aged 58.

"Call," daily newspaper; was founded on Dec. 1, 1856, by James J. Ayres, David W. Higgins, Lew Zublin, Chas. F. Jobson and W. L. Carpenter. It was purchased by the Bulletin proprietors, Messrs. Loring Pickering, Jas. W. Simonton and Geo. K. Fitch, in 1869; was sold by order of Court (to settle the partnership between Mr. Fitch and the estates of Messrs. Pickering and Simonton) Jan. 10, 1895, for $360,000, the purchaser being Chas. M. Shortridge, of San José, Cal.

Calvary Presbyterian Church was organized July 17, 1854; the building on north side Bush street, between Montgomery and Sansome, was dedicated in Dec., 1854; the present edifice, N. W. Powell and Geary streets, was dedicated in 1869.

Cameron, Caleb; one of the founders of the house of Cameron, Whittier & Co., paints, glass, oil, etc., in 1858, his partners being W. F. Whittier and E. B. Benjamin; the style was changed to Whittier, Fuller & Co. in 1867, and to W. P. Fuller & Co. in 1893. Mr. Cameron was drowned at Benicia, Nov. 26, 1861, leaving no family; his brother, a clergyman, succeeded to his estate, which was worth $40,000.

Cameron, J. Donald, Secretary of War, and Gen. W. T. Sherman, arrived Sept. 20, 1876.

Caminetti, McGee and Cavagnaro; law firm; was established in S. F. in Jan., 1891, and was dissolved in 1895. (Anthony Caminetti, J. F. Cavagnaro, and Wm. J. McGee.) Ex-Congressman Caminetti always maintained his residence in Jackson, Amador Co., where he was born, July 30, 1854, was admitted to the bar in May, 1877, and where he has won many public honors. He attended the S. F. public schools in boyhood.

Campbell, Alexander; was Judge of the 12th District Court, Jan., 1861 to 1862, when he resigned; was a School Director in 1863-64; he died at Oakland, Feb. 16, 1888, aged 79; a native of New Brunswick. A sketch of his life by O. T. S., is in the Bulletin, Feb. 17, 1888.

Campbell, Alexander; distinguished lawyer; a pioneer of Aug. 7, 1849; County Judge, 1851-52; removed to Arizona in 1881; settled in Los Angeles in 1886. A chapter in Bench and Bar narrates his extraordinary professional career. He was born on the island of Jamaica in 1820, of Scotch parents.

Campbell, Alex., Jr.; well-known lawyer, son of the preceding, was Assistant District Attorney under Hon. Wm. S. Barnes, 1890-91.

Campbell, Alvin C.; lawyer; pioneer of Aug., 1849; died of apoplexy, june 8, 1865, aged 40.

Campbell, James A.; Justice of the Peace, 1891-92; Judge of Police Court No. 1, three terms, 1893-98.

Campbell, J. W. H.; exhibited at the Paris Exposition of 1867, 120 pounds of California high mixed wheat, which he afterwards presented to the Royal Society of England.

Campbell, Thompson; distinguished orator and lawyer; was Secretary of State of Illinois in 1840; M. C. from that State, 1851-52, U. S. Land Commissioner for California, 1853; Chairman Judiciary Committee, California Assembly, 1863-64; died Dec. 6, 1868; a native of Penn., aged 56. (Sketch in Representative Men.)

Canby, Gen. E. R. S., U. S. A.; was treacherously murdered by Captain Jack in the Modoc war; his remains arrived from Portland, Oregon, en route to Indiana, May 12, 1873.

Canavan, P. H.; Supervisor, 1868-70; Member Board of Health, 1869; New City Hall Commissioner, 1870-74; died at Mayfield, June 5, 1882, native of Ireland, aged 52.

Cariboo Mines; the rush to, from S. F., occurred in Jan. and Feb., 1862.

Carmany, John H.; was born in Penn.; came to California in 1858; published the Commercial Herald in 1867; became owner of the Overland Monthly in 1868, and conducted it to its close, in 1875; lost $30,000 in this venture; was Supervisor from the Fourth Ward, 1882; engaged in mining, 1883 to 1886, when he retired from active business, establishing his residence in East Oakland. Mr. C. was an enterprising and discriminating publisher, and a friend to authors.

Caro, Alexander S.; Rabbi; died Aug. 29, 1885; aged 80.

Carpentier, Edward R.; a well-known lawyer, who amassed a considerable fortune in S. F., at an early day; was the close friend of Henry H. Byrne, who left him his estate of $90,000, less a few small legacies. Mr. C. returned to the State of N. Y., in 1881; he was born there in 1824. See Byrne, H. H.

Carpentier, Horace W.; brother of the preceding; a pioneer of Aug. 8, 1849; Enrolling Clerk, State Senate, elected Jan. 6, 1851; defeated for State Senate, by Elcan Heydenfeldt, Feb. 2, 1850; practiced law at S. F.; residing always in Oakland, until 1883, when he removed to N. Y.; visited S. F. in 1887, and testified (Aug. 11,) before the Pacific Railway Commission; again in July, 1893, and testified in suit of S. P. Company vs. Mayor Pardee of Oakland. See long article, with portrait, in Examiner, July 26, 1893; was born in N. Y., in 1822.

Carr, Jesse D.; pioneer of Aug. 18, 1849; represented S. F. in the Assembly, 2nd session, 1851; was President of the State Agricultural Society, 1885-86, being ex-officio, a regent of the State University; bought an extensive tract, eleven square leagues of land, of Thos.

O. Larkin's estate, in Monterey Co., March, 1860; had become a resident of that county some years prior; is one of the largest grain growers.

Carson, James G.; lawyer; was born in Ireland in 1844; came to S. F. in early childhood, with his parents. His father, Bernard Carson, was a card engraver, and died leaving a handsome estate. In 1866, when he was but twenty-two years old, he was the candidate of his party for Supervisor from the Ninth Ward and was defeated by A. J. Shrader; was a member of the Assembly at the session of 1875-76; died in S. F., May 2, 1888.

Carter, Chas. D.; pioneer of Aug. 28, 1849; Assistant Alderman, Oct. 1853 to Oct. 1854; President of the Board of Industrial School Directors, 1870-71; publisher of the "Real Estate Circular" from 1867 to his death; died May, 26, 1871, aged 46, a native of N. Y.

Cary, James C.; well-known lawyer; was Superior Judge in 1880, chosen at the first election under the Constitution of 1879; drew a one-year term.

Casebolt, Henry; projector and builder of the Sutter Street Railroad, sold a controlling interest in the road to Joseph Naphtaly and associates, for $143,000, Jan. 27, 1880.

Casey, James P.; foreman of Crescent Engine Co., No. 10 (of the old Volunteer Fire Dep't,) being charged by the Evening Bulletin with crime (said to have been committed in N. Y.) shot Mr. King, editor of the Bulletin, fatally, on the street, May 14, 1856; he was taken from the County Jail by the Great Vigilance Committee, and publicly hung, with Charles Cora, May 22, 1856.

Casserly, Eugene; distinguished lawyer; State Printer, 1851, elected by the legislature May 1, 1851; member of the 2nd Constitutional Convention, 1878-79; U. S. Senator, elected for six years beginning March 4, 1869; resigned Nov. 28, 1873; died at S. F., June 14, 1883; a native of Ireland, aged 61.

Catholic Churches: The Church of the Dominican Fathers, corner Bush and Steiner streets, was dedicated June 29, 1873.

Church of the Holy Cross, on Eddy street, was dedicated, April 20, 1873.

St. Francis, Vallejo street between Stockton and Dupont, was organized by Very Rev. Anthony Langlois and Right Rev. J. S. Alemany in the spring of 1849; the frame building was completed in Dec., 1849; the present brick edifice was dedicated on March 17, 1860. This was the first Catholic Church organized in S. F.

St. Mary's Church, N. E. corner California and Dupont streets, building was begun July 17, 1853; was opened by service at midnight Dec. 24, 1854; dedicated Dec. 25, 1854, by Most Rev. J. S. Alemany.

St. Mary's Cathedral, on Van Ness Avenue and O'Farrell street, the most magnificent church edifice in the State, was completed in 1890.

The Mission Dolores Church was organized Aug. 1, 1776; the building was completed and dedicated Oct. 8, 1776.

"Notre Dame des Victoires" was organized in May, 1856; the edifice North side Bush between Dupont and Stockton streets, was purchased from the Baptists, and dedicated May 4, 1856.

St. Ignatius Church, then on Market street between 4th and 5th, under the direction of the Jesuits, was dedicated July 15, 1855.

St. Ignatius Church and College buildings, corner Van Ness Avenue and Hayes street; the work of construction was begun by the Jesuit Fathers July 8, 1878; cornerstone was laid Oct. 20, 1878; the magnificent church edifice was dedicated in Feb., 1880. St. Ignatius College was organized as a day school, Oct. 15, 1855, and chartered as an incorporated college, April 30, 1859, under the direction of the Society of Jesus.

St. Patrick's Church on Mission street; corner stone was laid by Archbishop Alemany, Sept. 26, 1869; was presented with its melodious chime of bells by Peter Donahue, March 12, 1870.

The Spanish American Church was dedicated Dec. 26, 1875.

Catholics, Immense meeting of, to protest against the expulsion of Sisters of Charity from Mexico, was held Feb. 21, 1875.

Cavallier, J. B. E.; while President of the "Big" Board of Brokers, was presented by the Board with a silver punch bowl worth $1,600, Jan. 1, 1864; was Supervisor, 1868-69.

Cazotte, Charles de; Consul General of France; died of small pox, Feb. 13, 1869, aged 48.

Cazneau, Thomas N.; Port Warden, appointed by Gov. Bigler, 1851; Secretary State Senate, 1858; Immigration Commissioner, 1862; Adjutant Gen'l, appointed by Gov. Haight, Nov. 23, 1870; died July 11, 1873, a native of Mass., aged 61. There was an imposing funeral procession, with military features, July 13th. His regular business was that of insurance adjuster.

Cazneau, Wm. L.; father of the preceding, died at S. F., July 13, 1866, aged 97.

Cercle Français was organized April 12, 1884; incorporated June 9, 1888.

Centennial Celebration of the surrender of Cornwallis at Yorktown, Oct. 19, 1876; poem by Frank Soulé, read by Miss Nellie Holbrook.

Central Presbyterian Tabernacle, Golden Gate Avenue, was dedicated April 20, 1873.

Cemeteries: First interment was made in the grounds of the Catholic Church, Mission Dolores, in Sept., 1776.

Lone Mountain, or Laurel Hill Cemetery, was dedicated with a moving address by E. D. Baker, in June, 1854; first interment was on June 28th.

Calvary Cemetery was consecrated by Archbishop Alemany, with the rites of the Catholic Church, Aug. 17, 1862.

Chabot, Anthony; pioneer of July 18, 1849; was Sup't S. F. Water Works, 1859-60; removed to Oakland, 1861; Lake Chabot near that city, was named for him; presented Oakland with Chabot Observatory, in Lafayette Square; died at Oakland, Jan. 6, 1888; born in Canada in 1813; left an estate worth $1,348,370.

Chadwick, E. C. M.; popular captain of river steamers of California Steam Navigation Co.; died suddenly of heart disease, April 16. 1865.

Chaigneau, Victor; pioneer of April 16, 1849; miller of Genessee Flour Mills; died June 19, 1870.

Chain Gang, having been starved for sixty hours for refusing to work on the public streets, resumed work, and received rations, Nov. 26, 1858.

Chamber of Commerce was organized, May 6, 1851; dedication exercises and banquet in the new Merchants' Exchange building, Nov. 12, 1867.

Chamberlain, Chas. H.; Receiver of the U. S. Land Office, 1867 to Nov. 18, 1885; was State Senator from San Joaquin, 1862-63, and Assembly-man from same county, 1865-66; lawyer, and clever writer of humorous and pathetic verse.

Chamberlain, C. M.; was Supervisor in 1856.

Chambers, T. J. A.; pioneer of April 28, 1849; dealer in real estate and mining stocks, died Jan. 12, 1873, a native of Virginia, aged 68.

Chapelle, A. Marius; pioneer of July 25, 1849; real estate dealer, of some estate, committed suicide by jumping into the bay from an Oak-land ferry boat, Oct. 19, 1867; native of France, aged 57.

Chappelle, Jacob G.; veteran police detective; who was with Capt. Lees on the pilot boat Fanny, on the expedition to recover the secreted treasure of the ship Cornelia, on the Lower California Coast, April, 1858; his body was found in S. F. bay, a mysterious death, Dec. 17, 1872.

Chapman, Miss Caroline; of the celebrated Chapman theatrical family, died May 8, 1876.

Chapman, George; noted early day actor, died Nov. 16, 1876, aged 73.

Chapman, Mary; relict of Geo. Chapman, famous actor; herself a popular actress; died March 1, 1880; born in N. Y. City, June 13, 1815; ar-rived in California, 1851.

Chapman, Wm. S.; great land lord and speculator; is largely interested in gold mining, and has written much on the subject; an interest-ing interview with him is in the Bulletin of June 29, 1893; a communication by him, on "Gold Mining," is in same paper of July 20, 1893, in which he expressed the wish that the State had "one thousand Alvinza Haywards;" a daughter of his is the wife of a son of Gen. U. S. Grant. Mr. C. registered, Aug. 2, 1866, as a native of Ohio, aged 39.

Charters for the City and County, prepared by four different Boards of Freeholders, elected by the people, were defeated: the first, March 30, 1880; 2nd, March 5, 1883; 3rd, April 12, 1887; 4th, Nov. 3, 1896. For the names of the Freeholders and the popular vote at each election, see Supplement.

Chenery, Chas E.; commercial editor of the Chronicle, died Dec. 17, 1876.

Chenery, Richard; pioneer of Aug. 14, 1849; Assemblyman, 1857; U. S.

Návy Agent, 1862-65; President of the California pioneers, 1869-70; died at Belfast, Maine, July 27, 1890; a native of Mass., aged 73.

Cheney, John Vance; poet, essayist, and literary critic; was a clerk in the P. O., 1887, and was librarian of the Free Public Library, 1888 to 1895, when he resigned, and removed to Chicago.

Cherry, John W.; County Recorder, 1882; registered July 2, 1866, as a native of N. J., aged 38; was a member of Assembly, 1858; 1859; 1861; 1863-64; while President of the Exempt Firemen, he died at Paterson, N. J., in 1885, aged 57.

Chevallier, J. B.; esteemed citizen and teacher of languages, died Nov. 28, 1870.

Chevers, Wm. H.; Court Commissioner 15th District Court, died June 17, 1877.

Chickering, Thomas & Gregory; leading law firm; was formed in 1892; to that year, from 1878, it was Chickering & Thomas (Wm. H. Chickering and William Thomas); the style was changed to Olney, Chickering & Thomas in 1885; after seven years, Warren Olney withdrew and Warren Gregory entered, (C., T. & G.). Theac cession of Marcus L. Gerstle and Marcus C. Sloss was in 1895, when the style became Chickering, Thomas & Gregory, and Gerstle & Sloss. The firm name was restored to Chickering, Thomas & Gregory, (Messrs. Gerstle and Sloss continuing in the partnership) Feb. 20, 1897.

Childs, James; pioneer stevedore; died Sept. 28, 1869, aged 42.

China and Japan steamship line; was inaugurated with a grand banquet at the Occidental Hotel, Dec. 31, 1866.

Chinese; The Burlingame Treaty, was our third treaty with China, and was ratified in 1868.

The voters of the State, pursuant to an Act of the legislature of Dec. 21, 1877, expressed their judgment on the question of Chinese immigration, at the general election in 1879; those declaring in favor of such immigration numbered 883; those opposed numbered 154,638.

The Ten Years Exclusion Act was passed in May, 1882.

The Scott Exclusion Act was passed in Oct., 1888; excluding all Chinese laborers from this country.

The Geary (Registration) Act was passed May 5, 1892.

The U. S. Supreme Court declared this Act to be constitutional, on May 15, 1893.

"Chinese Six Companies, The;" article by Richard Hay Drayton, appeared in "The Californian Magazine," for Aug., 1893.

"Our Treaties with China," with (reflections on our legislation with regard to the Chinese); article by Frederick J. Masters, D. D., is in "The Californian Magazine," for Aug., 1893.

"The Law and the Chinaman;" article by ex-Congressman Thos. J. Geary, is in "The Californian Magazine," for July, 1893.

Chinese, over 300 in number, formed part of the procession on Independence Day, 1852; they carried a large silk flag, costing $2000, a Chinese band of music was in a carriage, making "horrible harmony;" Mandarins, (at least so called) were in carriages and on horse.

Chinese Mission House was organized by Rev. Wm. Speer, Presbyterian missionary, Feb. 13, 1853; the building N. E. corner Sacramento and Stockton streets, was dedicated on the fourth Sabbath in June, 1854.

"Whole cargoes of Chinese," (an expression used at the time) arrived in July, 1854, and were landed, on account of the scurvy among them, on Goat Island, where they died in large numbers.

A "Protest against Chinese Cooleyism," with 11,000 signatures, was sent to the legislature Jan. 30, 1860.

Chinese laborers, excavating a lot on Townsend street near Second, were driven from their work, and their shanties destroyed, by a white mob, which next proceeded to the Potrero and drove off the Chinese employed at the rope walk of Tubbs & Co., setting fire to their cabins, Feb. 12, 1867; the leaders of the riot were apprehended, and sentenced each to 90 days imprisonment and $500 fine, Feb. 28, 1867; an immense anti-coolie meeting was held at the American Theater, March 6, 1867.

Chinese Embassy, arrived on the steamship "China," March 31, 1868; banqueted by American merchants at the Lick House, April 28th; visited the Harbor fortifications, in company with Gen. Halleck and Admiral Thatcher, April 29th.

Chinese Theater on Jackson street near Dupont, was formally opened, and a grand banquet given, attended by a large number of American and Chinese guests, Jan. 27, 1868.

Chung Lock; a powerful Chinese merchant, died Aug. 30, 1868, aged 53.

There was a riot among the Chinese, and several were wounded, April 17, 1870.

A serious fight occurred between rival Chinese cigar makers, on Battery street, April 8, 1870.

Chinese testimony was admitted in the County Court, March 24, 1870.

300 Chinese laborers left for Minnesota on contract, April 29, 1870; several hundred had gone to Texas, on contract, some months prior; Chinamen in large numbers, engaged in rioting, at a joss house, several receiving serious injuries, May 22, 1870; 1200 Chinese laborers left for Georgia, on contract, July 8, 1870; great anti-Chinese meeting at Platt's Hall, same night; two Chinamen were arrested, charged with counterfeiting bills of the Bank of India, July 12, 1870.

The Chinese Mission Institute (Presbyterian), corner Washington and Stone streets, was dedicated Dec. 25, 1870; a Chinaman was stoned and beat to death by a gang of boys, May 31, 1871.

There was a fracas between Chinamen, resulting in one death, June 26, 1871.

A meeting of laboring men was held to petition the U. S. Senate in favor of a law prohibiting immigration of Chinese laborers, Oct. 5, 1871.

Chinese testimony was admitted by Police Judge Louderback, Jan. 3, 1872.

A petition to Congress, asking a modification of the treaty with China, so as to stop the influx of Chinese, was numerously signed, in May, 1873.

Forty-five Chinamen found sleeping in one room, were arrested on a charge of violating the health laws, May 20, 1873.

The Chinese Six Companies telegraphed to Hong Kong, to have emigration to this port stopped, May 28, 1873.

A large anti-Chinese meeting was held at Dashaway Hall, May 29, 1873.

Mayor Alvord vetoed several anti-Chinese ordinances, June 9, 1873.

Twenty-eight Chinese students arrived by steamer, en route to Springfield, Mass., July 13, 1873, there to pursue English studies.

A picnic of Chinese Sunday School children was held at Woodward's Gardens, July 31, 1874.

The old First Baptist Church edifice, on North side Washington street, East of Stockton, was purchased by Chinese merchants, for store and lodging uses, May 28, 1875.

A furious affray occurred among the Chinese, knives being freely used, March 4, 1875.

Fifty Chinamen attacked a Chinese mercantile house, and seven were wounded, Feb. 29, 1876.

A public meeting of prominent citizens, to discuss the Chinese question, was held March 26, 1876.

A special committee of twelve citizens, appointed by the Board of Supervisors, met to consider the Chinese problem, March 22, 1876.

The Chinese inhabitants became generally alarmed at the popular anti-Chinese feeling, March 30, 31, 1876; the Six Companies issuing a manifesto to the American people.

The Six Companies petitioned the Board of Supervisors for protection, April 3, 1876.

The whites, in mass meeting at Union Hall, called for the repeal of the Burlingame Treaty, April 5, 1876.

Einstein & Co., boot and shoe manufacturers, discharged 300 Chinese employees, April 6, 1876.

A Senatorial Chinese Investigation Commission convened at S. F., April 11, 1876.

An attack by a mob on the Chinese passengers arriving on the ship "Crocus," was prevented by the police, on Easter Sunday, April 16, 1876.

District Judge S. B. McKee, decided the ordinance imposing a special tax upon Chinese laundries to be unconstitutional, May 2, 1876.

The ordinance providing for cutting off the hair of prisoners
in the County Jail (aimed in spirit but not in letter at the Chinese), was enforced by cutting off the queue of a Chinese convicted of misdemeanor, June 3, 1876.

There was a conflict between whites and Chinese on Clay
street near Battery, with no serious result, June 22, 1876.

An alarm of fire at the Chinese Theater on Jackson street
caused a panic, Oct. 31, 1876; 19 Chinamen were killed, and 12
wounded.

A Congressional Chinese Commission, composed of U. S. Sen-
ators Oliver P. Morton and A. A. Sargent, and Representatives
Piper, Cooper and Mead, began their investigation at S. F., Oct.
17, 1876; this Commission adjourned, Nov. 18, 1876.

The various trade Unions had a large anti-Chinese procession
and a great meeting at the Mechanics' Pavillon, Nov. 18, 1876;
Mayor Bryant presiding.

Miss Fannie Waters, a governess, a native of Maine, aged 21,
was married to Ah Wah, a Chinese laundryman, by Rev. Mr.
Loomis, Presbyterian, Nov. 16, 1876.

The Anti-Coolie Convention assembled July 5, 1877.

After a mass meeting of workingmen, to express sympathy
with the Eastern strikers, several Chinese wash houses were
wrecked by hoodlums, July 23, 1877.

Gangs of hoodlums burned some Chinese wash houses, and
wrecked others, July 24, 1877; on that day the National Guard was
put on duty at the Armories, and citizens formed a Committee of
Safety.

Mayor Bryant issued a proclamation appealing to the people to
support the law, July 25, 1877; on the same day several hundred
citizens were sworn in as special policemen; there were incendiary
fires in the lumber yards near the city front, South of Market
street, causing a loss of $100,000; collisions followed between the
white rioters on one side and the Citizens' Committee of Safety,
the police, and the National Guard on the other, and the rioters
sacked several wash houses; the Mayor issued a second proclamation the same day; on the day following, July 26th, over 4000 men
were put on police duty; Joseph Smith was arrested for arson, and
on July 27th he was held in $20,000 bail by the Police Judge, who
imposed heavy sentences on other rioters.

The Committe of Safety disbanded, July 30, 1877.

Levi's wool-dyeing establishment, corner Brannan and Eleventh streets, was destroyed by a mob, Aug. 2, 1877.

Attempts were made to burn the residence of Wm. T. Coleman,
Aug. 3, 1877.

The boots and shoes manufacturers organized against Chinese
labor, March 12, 1878.

Judge Lorenzo Sawyer, of the U. S. District Court, held that
Chinamen were not eligible to citizenship, April 29, 1878.

COUNCIL CHAMBER OF THE SIX COMPANIES, SAN FRANCISCO.

Chinese Embassy arrived on the "City of Tokio," July 26, 1878.

The right of Chinese to fish in the waters of the State, was sustained by U. S. Circuit Judge Lorenzo Sawyer, the State Constitution and laws to the contrary notwithstanding, June, 1880. (Opinion in full in Bulletin, June 9, 1880.)

"Chinatown" was condemned as a nuisance by the Board of Health, Feb. 21, 1880, the condemned district being bounded by Stockton, Kearny, California, and Broadway streets.

A long editorial on the labor situation in S. F., appeared in the London Times, Feb. 20, 1880.

On March 4, 1880, the Presidents of the Chamber of Commerce and Cotton Exchange at New Orleans, telegraphed to W. F. Babcock, President of the Chamber of Commerce at S. F., that the Chinese of S. F. could find profitable employment in the sugar cotton, and rice fields of Louisiana.

Tiburcio Parrott, President of the Sulphur Bank Quicksilver Co., was arrested Feb. 20, 1880, for violating the law of Feb. 13, 1880, prohibiting corporations from employing Chinese; the U. S. Circuit Court granted a writ of *habeas corpus*, Feb. 21, 1880, the petition alleging that the Act was unconstitutional, and in contravention of the Burlingame Treaty; the Sulphur Bank Co. discharged all its Chinese employees, Feb. 24, 1880, while this case was pending, the Superintendent having requested it, because of the hostile feeling on the part of the public.

The Act of the legislature prohibiting the employment of Chinese by corporations, became a law, Feb. 13, 1880; this Act added two sections to the Penal Code, sections 178 and 179, and punished by a fine not less than $100 nor more than $1,000, or by an imprisonment in the County Jail for not less than 50 days nor more than 500 days, or by both such fine and imprisonment, any officer of any corporation formed in this State, who should employ any Chinese upon any corporation work or business.

The Mission and Pioneer Woolen Mills discharged their Chinese workmen, Feb. 17, 1880.

The Great Western Quicksilver Co., of Lake Co., discharged all its Chinese employees, Feb. 17, 1880; this was in compliance with the just enacted law prohibiting corporations from employing Chinese labor; the company also suspended operations on account of the high price of white labor.

A careful canvass at Sacramento, in the middle of February, 1880, showed that not a single Chinaman was employed by any of the corporations, excepting a solitary interpreter at the railroad depot.

The Supervisors passed an ordinance in May, which took effect June 10, 1882, aimed at the Chinese, making it unlawful to conduct any laundry in that portion of the city East of Larkin and Ninth streets, without the consent of the Board and the recommendation of 12 citizens and tax payers; this ordinance was held to be unconstitutional by U. S. Judges Field and Sawyer, Aug., 1882.

The "Bingham Ordinance," passed by the Supervisors in 1890, providing for restricting the Chinese population of the city, in their business and residence, to certain defined territorial limits, was declared by U. S. Circuit Judge Sawyer to be unconstitutional, and in conflict with the Burlingame Treaty, Aug. 25, 1890.

"A Stain on the Flag" (Chinese Slavery in America); article by Mrs. M. G. C. Edholm in the Californian Magazine for Feb. 1892.

The Chinese Exclusion Act was approved May 5, 1892; it provided that all Chinese laborers must procure certificates of residence before May 6, 1893, and by affirmative proof must establish their right to remain in this country.

Ming Lee Twe, the first Chinese deported under the Geary Exclusion Act, departed on the steamship Rio de Janeiro, Aug. 10, 1893; he was ordered deported by U. S. District Judge Ross at Los Angeles; his fare was paid by a voucher of the U. S. Government for $35.

"A Chinese Protest against Exclusion," article by John Bonner in The Californian Magazine for April, 1894.

The usual bedlam in the Chinese quarter, attendant upon the observance of Chinese New Year, Feb. 1-8, 1897, was entirely prohibited by the Chief of Police; and a strong police force was kept on patrol to enforce the order, effectually preventing the discharge of bombs and fire crackers. This was without precedent, and was occasioned by threatened sanguinary frays among the heathen, consequent upon the murder of "Little Pete," a Chinaman of great influence, by men of his own race, in the middle of January.

Chipman, Gen. John S.; ex-M. C. from Michigan, was arrested for alleged treasonable utterances in a public speech, and conveyed to Alcatraz, May 6, 1864; was released May 25th.

Chosen Friends, Order of; the Grand Council was organized, May 17, 1881.

Chretien John M.; lawyer; was born in S. F., Aug. 29, 1853; graduated from Santa Clara College in 1872; admitted to the bar of the Supreme Court in 1875.

Christian work, Society for; was organized Oct., 1873, in connection with the First Unitarian Church.

Chronicle, Dramatic, was issued first on Jan. 27, 1865. The word *Dramatic* was dropped, Aug. 18, 1868.

"Chronicle"-"Sun," libel controversy—see local papers, Feb. 17, 1874, and near dates.

Chittenden, N. W.; able and wealthy lawyer; was born in N. Y., in 1818; died in Watsonville, Cal., Nov. 23, 1885; was admitted to the bar in N. Y.; settled in S. F., Aug. 18, 1849; practiced in S. F. for thirty years; during nearly all that long period he had his office and residence in the granite building N. W. corner Montgomery and Jackson streets; was a bachelor with no kin in this State; a cultured man, of courtly bearing, but reticent; left all his estate, worth about $125,000, to Robert Simson, of Alameda, who was his business partner, and who had been his law partner (C. & S.) in 1877-78.

Church Extension Society of Methodist Church was organized in 1882.

Church, Edward W.; of Sather & Church, bankers; died April 29, 1861.

Cincinnati Commercial Party; arrived on a tour of inspection and pleasure, Sep. 10, 1869.

"City Gardens" were first opened to the public, July 21, 1867.

"City Gardens," corner of Folsom and 12th streets, were sold Feb. 12, 1877, for $192,500.

City Hall lots, owned by the city, were sold at auction, realizing $954,900, Aug. 28, 1871.

City Hall; the City Hall Commissioners transferred the books, property, etc., pertaining to the New City Hall, to the Board of Supervisors, April 29, 1874, at 3 P. M.; the Commissioners being P. H. Canavan, Jos. G. Eastland and Chas. E. McLane.

City Hall; the principal Municipal offices were moved into the new building on McAllister and Larkin streets, July 1, 1878.

"City Slip;" was a term applied in the Fifties to the water-covered area, since embraced within Clay, Sacramento, Davis and East streets. It had been left open for the purposes of navigation. The City sold it, in lots 25x59 9-12, in Dec., 1853. The important ten years litigation which followed between the purchasers and the city, ended in a compromise in 1863, and is noticed in Bench and Bar in California, pages 29-30.

Civil Rights Act; Thos. Maguire, theatrical manager, was tried for refusing to admit Chas. Green, colored, to his theater, and was acquitted Jan. 18, 1876.

Clarke, Alfred, Jr.; was Superintendent of the Fire Alarm, etc., Jan. 30-Feb. 27, 1888.

Clarke, Newman S.; Brevet Brig.-Gen'l commmanding the Department of the Pacific, died Oct. 17, 1860; obsequies were observed on the 18th, with great pomp.

Clarke, Robert; Captain of ship Sunrise, found guilty on seven counts of cruelty to his crew, Oct. 28, 1873; was sentenced Nov. 28, 1873, to 14 months' imprisonment in the County Jail and $1000 fine; Frank Harris, his first mate, was sentenced to four years in State prison; Dennis Maloney, 2d mate, to two months in County Jail; Maloney died in County Hospital, Dec. 22, 1873.

Clark, Isabella; a Moorish fortune teller, who came into prominence in connection with the Sharon divorce suit, died at the Almshouse, Oct. 2, 1885, a native of Jerusalem, Holy Land, aged 90 years.

Clark, Reuben; the first architect of the State Capitol, who was referred to in a legislative joint commission as "an architect of vast experience and pre-eminent upon this coast," died in 1866; a pioneer of Aug. 18, 1849.

Clark, Wm. S.; pioneer of Oct., 1846; died at San José, Nov 16, 1883; a

native of Maryland, aged 82; sketch in Bulletin Nov. 28th; for
Sarah M. Reed's suit against him for breach of promise, see 47
Cal., 194; and see Haggin vs. Clark, 51 Cal., 112.

Claughly, Mrs. Mary; actress; died of typhus fever, Aug. 21, 1864.

Clay Street Railroad; from Kearny to Leavenworth, was constructed in
1873; was extended to Van Ness Avenue in 1878; was the pioneer
road in the use of the endless wire cable, invented and patented
by A. S. Hallidie, of S. F.

Clayton, Charles; influential and esteemed citizen; Member Board of
Health, 1866-67; Supervisor two terms, 1865-68; Member of Congress, March 4, 1873-March 4, 1875; died at Oakland, Oct. 4, 1885.

Clearing House; bankers held a meeting and resolved to establish one,
Dec. 15, 1875; met again and passed a like resolution, Feb. 4, 1876;
the Clearing house began business March 8, 1876.

Clemens, Samuel; (" Mark Twain"); for notice of, see "Some California
Writers," in The Californian, for May, 1893.

Clement Grammar School (Public); was named Sept. 18, 1877, after Joseph
Clement, a pioneer of 1849, who was a member of the Board of
Education five consecutive terms—1870-79—and President of the
Board in 1872-73 and in 1876-77.

Clement, Henry N.; well-known lawyer; was a Member of the Board of
Freeholders which framed the proposed City Charter that was
defeated at the general election, Nov. 3, 1896.

Clement, R. P.; well-known lawyer; was Supervisor in 1866-67; is a native
of N. Y., born in 1826; a sketch of his life is in Bancroft's Contemporary Biography.

Clement, Jabish; a promising young lawyer of S. F., brother of R. P. Clement, died suddenly in Oregon, while visiting there, in April, 1874.

Cliff House; time honored place of resort; the old building was erected in
1863; was opened Oct. 15th, with J. G. Foster as proprietor; C. C.
Butler owned the property; Mr. Foster was succeeded by McCrum
& Sheldon in 1884; in 1885, G. E. Sheldon; 1886, R. C. Pearson;
1887, A. Wilkins; 1890, Peter Formey; 1892, Jas. M. Wilkins; 1895,
Wilkins & Pearson. The property was bought by Adolph Sutro,
of Butler, Austin, and the Buckley heirs, in 1870; the old building
was burned Christmas Day, 1894; the present splendid structure
was opened in Feb., 1896; Colley & Lemme, architects.

Clift, Frederick C.; the honored Justice of the Peace in Oakland, who has
held that office since Jan., 1893, qualified himself for the bar in S.
F., in the office of, first, Nathaniel Bennett, and after the latter's
death, in that of P. D. Wigginton. He was born in Grass Valley,
Cal., July 20, 1867, and was admitted to the bar at Sacramento,
May 6, 1890.

Clinton, Dr. Chas. A.; prominent physician; was a member of the Board of
Health in 1888; School Director, 1893-94; Supervisor, 1897-98.

Clifford, George; an old pioneer; died Jan 5, 1877.

Clough, F. M.; Justice of the Peace, 1881-82; Superior Judge, 1883-85; resigned the latter office on Aug. 23, 1885; died at the Insane Asylum

at Stockton, Feb. 14, 1888; a native of San José, Cal., aged 33 years, 6 months; his funeral was conducted by the N. S. G. W.

Cluff, Richard; senior brother of Cluff Brothers, wholesale grocers, died Feb. 4, 1883, from injuries received in being thrown from a buggy in Golden Gate Park, Jan. 30, 1883; native of Ireland, aged 53; funeral from Howard street Methodist Church.

Clunie, Andrew J.; a lawyer of wide and well-earned reputation; was Assistant City and County Attorney. in 1887; came to S. F. from Sacramento, in 1883, was a student in the office of his brother, Gen. Thos. J. Clunie, with whom he immediately entered into partnership, upon being admitted to the bar in 1887.

Clunie, Thos. J.; prominent and wealthy lawyer; removed to S. F. from Sacramento in 1881; was in the Assembly from Sacramento, 1875-76; State Senator from S. F., 1887; Member of Congress, March 4, 1889-March 4, 1891. Having acquired while yet a minor a large property by real estate operations in Sacramento following the great flood, he was declared of lawful age by Act of the legislature of March 4, 1868. His fine Opera House in Sacramento was opened in 1885.

Coal from Coos Bay, Oregon, was first introduced to the S. F. market, Jan., 1856.

Cobb, M. G.: prominent lawyer, was born in Mass., Nov. 24, 1820; was shot and slightly wounded by Hannah Smythe on the street in Jan., 1875; she was acquitted, as insane, April 29, 1875.

Cobb, Wm. H., located, and began law practice, in S. F. in Jan., 1890; was born in Iowa, Aug. 18, 1860; graduated from the University of Iowa, the classical course in 1883, the law course in 1886.

Cockrill, Theo. G.; was Chief of Police, 1874-75. Sketch in Bancroft's "Contemporary Biography."

Cocos Island treasure hunters returned to port disappointed, July 27, 1876.

Coey, James; a colonel in the war of the Rebellion, enlisting in N. Y.; Postmaster in S. F., 1869-70; commissioned Brig.-Gen'l, N. G. C., by Gov. Pacheco, Jan. 5, 1875; President of the Day at the Centennial celebration, July 4, 1876; registered June 24, 1867, as a native of N. Y., aged 26.

Coffey, James V.; Judge in the Probate Department of the Superior Court since Sep., 1883; was born in N. Y. City, Dec. 14, 1846; awarded the great estate of Thos. H. Blythe to Miss Florence, as the only child and heir of the deceased millionaire, July 31, 1890, the Supreme Court affirming his judgment. A volume of his opinions, reported by T. J. Lyons and Edmund Tauszky, was issued by those gentlemen in 1888. Judge C. was first elected Superior Judge in 1882; was presiding Judge in 1887; was re-elected Superior Judge in Nov., 1894, for six years from Jan., 1895; was an Assemblyman, 1875-76, and 1877-78, being Chairman of the S. F. delegation at both sessions; he was Secretary of the Board of Port Wardens, 1869-72, and has been President of the California Historical Society, since 1893; he was defeated by M. A. Edmonds for

Superior Judge by one majority, 1880; the Supreme Court decision, on the contest for the office, is in Bulletin, Aug. 13, 1881.

Coffey, W. H.; brother of Hon. James V. Coffey, and connected with the Tide Land Survey, fell, fatally stricken from heart disease, Aug. 11, 1871.

Coffey & Risdon's Boiler Works were established by Thos. Snow, in May, 1853, and were purchased by C. & R. in July, 1855.

Coffin, Zenas; well-known civil engineer, died suddenly, Oct. 26, 1874.

Cofran, George; who was School Director in 1859 and in 1861-62, and Superintendent of Streets, 1864-68; died May 4, 1885, a native of N. H., aged 69 years, 6 months.

Cohen, Alfred A.; capitalist, and a lawyer of great ability; was born in London, England, July 17, 1829; died on the railroad train, near Sydney, Nebraska, while returning from N. Y. to S. F., Nov. 16, 1887; he sold the S. F. and Alameda R. R. Co's line to the Central Pacific R. R. Co.; a bitter controversy with the magnates of the latter company followed, and lasted several years, their complaint, for $106,306, damages, being filed in the 12th District Court, March 7, 1876; for his own story of his railroad connections, see the local press, Aug. 22, 1876.

Cohen, Frederick A.; brother of the preceding; assaulted Thos. S. King, editor of the Bulletin, Feb. 12, 1857.

Coit, Dr. Benjamin B.; distinguished physician, fell dead on the street, from heart disease, April 16, 1867.

Coit, Mrs. H. H.; widow of Dr. B. B. Coit, and mother of B. Howard Coit, died at Annadale, N. J., in 1885.

Coit, B. Howard; Caller of the S. F Stock and Exchange Board, died of heart disease during sleep, May 14, 1885; a native of N. Y., aged 47; was elected caller of the Stock Board in 1870, and his remarkable aptitude for the position, secured him a salary of $1000 a month. He married Miss Lily, daughter of Dr. C. M. Hitchcock, who survived him.

Cole, R. Beverly; distinguished physician and surgeon since early times; Professor of Obstetrics in Medical Department, University of the Pacific, 1862; Supervisor for the 4th Ward, 1868-69; delegate to the Triennial Conclave of Knights Templar at St. Louis, Sept., 1886; registered Aug. 1, 1872, as a native of Virginia, aged 37. A celebrated observation of his about the women of California, raised a storm of criticism in Jan., 1859; the Dr. was brought to trial by the State Medical Society; made explanation and disclaimer; was exculpated by a vote of 22 to 8; see Bulletin, Jan. 10; Feb. 11, 14, 1859.

Colfax, Schuyler; Vice President of the U. S., arrived on his second visit to S. F., Aug. 13, 1869; visited the State a third time in June, 1878, lecturing in S. F. on Abraham Lincoln, June 15.

College of the Law, Hastings, was founded by S. Clinton Hastings, March 26, 1878. See Hastings, S. C.

Coleman, Wm. T.; pioneer of Aug. 4, 1849; President of the great Vigilance Committees of 1851, and 1856, and of the Citizens' Committee of Safety, 1877; President of the Pioneers, Oct., 1876-July, 1877; bought the Forbes' property at San Rafael, for $40,000, Oct. 15, 1885; sold his city residence, S. W. Washington and Taylor streets, to D. M. Delmas, for the same amount, 1890; died Nov. 22, 1893, aged 69; a native of Kentucky. Sketches in "Representative Men," and Bancroft's "Contemporary Biography."

Colmere, Geo. W.; under sentence of death for wife murder, committed suicide in his cell, by opening a vein in his arm with the tooth of a haircomb, Feb. 5, 1864.

"Colon," Peruvian Dispatch Boat; an attempt to seize it in S. F. bay; Daniel E. Hungerford, A. A. C. Williams, W. W. Bruce, Louis de la Nord, William Burns, Wm. B. Clarke, John Thomas, and Titus Reynolds, were arrested May 31, 1865, and were held in bail of $2,500 each, Jan. 6, 1865; acquitted by jury, July 15, 1865. Col. Hungerford was the father of Mrs. Jno. W. Mackay.

Colorado Steam Navigation Co., was incorporated Jan. 12, 1864.

Colored Methodists organized Zion M. E. Church, with Rev. John J. Moore as pastor, Aug. 1, 1852.

Colored Men, six in number, were drawn on a jury in the U. S. Circuit Court, Feb. 12, 1872; the first instance of the kind in the State.

Colton, David D.; lawyer and wealthy citizen; financial director of the great railroad system of the Coast, and President of the Occidental and Oriental Steamship Co., died Oct. 11, 1878, of blood poisoning, his case being a strange one, of which the surgeon, Dr. C. C. Keeney, U. S. A., published a statement; Gen. Colton was born in Maine, July 17, 1831; he was a second of Broderick in the duel with Terry, Sept., 1859.

Colton, Ellen M.; widow of Gen. D. D.; her great suit against Leland Stanford et al., before Superior Judge Jackson Temple of Sonoma Co., was decided in favor of the defendants, Oct. 6, 1885; affirmed by the Supreme Court—five Justices concurring, and two not participating. For the decision, see S. F. papers, Jan. 2, 1890.

Colton residence on Nob Hill; an object of general admiration, was built by Gen. David D. Colton, at a cost of $75,000, in 1872; the design, or picture, of the original was brought from Europe by ex-U. S. Senator Milton S. Latham, in 1868. This property was bought from Gen. Colton's widow by C. P. Huntington for $250,000 in 1892. Long prior thereto, on the night of Feb. 2, 1870, the mansion was visited by burglars, who carried off a large amount of silverware.

Columbus Banking Company was incorporated March 10, 1893.

"Comanche," an iron-clad monitor of the U. S. Navy, was successfully launched Nov. 14, 1864; Hon. John P. Buckley, an esteemed citizen was fatally injured.

"Comet of 1858;" E. D. Baker's glowing Apostrophe is in "California Anthology;" the address which contains it is in full in the "California Scrap Book."

Commercial Bank, The; suspended Dec. 24, 1875, after a short life; its place of business was at 421 California street.

Commissioners of the Funded Debt of 1855, were D. J. Tallant, John Middleton, Wm. Hooper, Wm. M. Lent, and Henry Haight.

"Committee of One Hundred;" was organized by prominent citizens to oppose the cession of Goat Island to the railroad companies; held their first meeting April 17, 1872.

Common Law of England. See Crittenden, A. P.

Comstock Lode; first receipt of silver ore from, amounting to four tons, valued at $7,000, was shipped to France, Oct. 20, 1859.

Comte, A., Jr.; prominent lawyer; Assemblyman from Sacramento, 1867-68; State Senator, 1869-72; removed to S. F. in 1873, abandoning the law for a season, to enter the wholesale liquor firm of F. Chevalier & Co.; was manager of the French Savings Bank, 1877-80; returned to the legal profession in 1881, and has since that date been attorney for the bank named, and has had a heavy probate practice; was a member of the Board of Freeholders to frame a City Charter, 1880; School Director, 1895-96; was born in St. Louis, Mo., Sept. 25, 1842; and is a graduate of Harvard College.

Concordia Club was organized Nov. 1864.

Coney, Rosalia L. de; wife of Hon. Alexander K. Coney, Consul for Mexico, died Feb. 18, 1897; a native of Mexico, aged 52; funeral from the Spanish Catholic Church.

Coney, Alexander K.; has been Consul General at S. F., for Mexico, since 1885.

Confederate Privateer "Chapman;" fitted out in S. F. bay; was captured in the harbor, March 15, 1863; Greathouse, Rubery and Harpending were found guilty, Oct. 13, 1863; R. was pardoned by President Lincoln, Jan. 20, 1864; G. was released, on taking oath under amnesty proclamation, and the prize money realized from a sale of the "Chapman" was distributed by order of Court, Jan. 26, 1864; H. was released on taking the oath, March 3, 1864.

Congregational Church, First; was organized July 29, 1849; the frame building, corner Jackson and Virginia streets, was dedicated Feb. 10, 1850; the brick edifice S. W. California and Dupont streets was dedicated July 10, 1853; brick edifice S. E. Post and Mason streets, dedicated May 19, 1872; cost, including the site, $150,000.

Congregation Emanu-El, (Hebrew) was founded in April, 1851; dedicated its fine synagogue on Sutter street, in 1866.

Congregational Ministers' Relief Society was incorporated in 1886.

Congressional Committee of Ways and Means, arrived June 23, 1869.

Conlan, Chas. T.; Police Judge of S. F. since Jan., 1893, (three terms) was born at Sacramento, Cal., Sept. 6, 1864; admitted to the bar at that place, May 4, 1886; educated at Santa Clara College.

Connely, D. W.; pioneer of Sept. 1, 1879; Member of Assembly, 1867-68; Park Commissioner, 1870-72; died in the latter office, Jan. 21, 1872; a native of Virginia, aged 66.

Connelly, J. D.; Justice of the Peace, 1880-82; fell from the window of his

Court room, S. E. corner Kearny and Washington streets, and was instantly killed, June 1, 1882.

Connell, Chas. D.; ex-Assistant Engineer of the Fire Department, dropped dead, April 1, 1871.

Conroy, M. C.; Sergeant-at-Arms of the Assembly, 1873-74; License Collector, 1885-87; died in office Feb. 4, 1887; registered, May 22, 1866, as a Post Office clerk, native of N. Y., aged 34.

Consolidation Act; Uniting the City of San Francisco and the County of San Francisco under one Municipal Government, was approved April 19, 1856; Horace Hawes was the author of this important measure. It took effect July 1, 1856.

Constitutional Convention of 1878-79; the election of delegates took place on June 19, 1878; with six tickets in the field the Kearney Workingmen elected their nominees by an average majority of 5385 over the Non Partisans. (The Non Partisans, however, organized the State Convention by one majority.)

Contra Costa Laundry; the Contra Costa Laundry was established by J. C. Davis, on what is now known as Laundry Farm, in Alameda County, A. D., 1855; in 1861 he sold to W. H. Bovee; during the freshet of 1862 the place was rendered useless, when the laundry was removed to Oakland, where it has since been. The laundry was incorporated in 1892; and is a close corporation, the stock being held by G. H. Hallett, P. Bartlett, and P. E. Dalton.

Convent of St. Rose; corner stone was laid on July 22, 1877; the convent was dedicated on April 14, 1878.

Cook, Elisha; distinguished lawyer; born in N. Y., Aug. 27, 1823; located in S. F. in 1850; counsel for the first great Vigilance Committee, 1851; married the second daughter of Wm. C. Hoff, Jan. 10, 1854; died Dec. 31, 1871. Sketch in Evening Post, Sept. 9, 1882.

Cook, Carroll; son of the preceding; prominent at the bar in notable criminal cases for many years; was elected Judge of the Superior Court, Nov. 2, 1896, for a full term of six years, ending in Jan., 1903; was Assistant U. S. District Attorney, 1883-85; registered on June 1, 1896, as a native of California, aged 41.

Cook, Josiah; distinguished lawyer; brother of Elisha Cook; practiced in S. F. from Jan., 1855 to July, 1857, when he returned to Buffalo, N. Y., where he had been admitted to the bar, Nov. 7, 1853; he was born in N. Y., July 13, 1824.

Cook, Isaac; a member of the pioneer banking firm of Palmer, Cook & Co., died Jan. 9, 1880; a native of Mass., aged 54; Masonic burial.

Cook, G. W. F.; who has been a Justice of the Peace since Jan., 1891, having been regularly elected for four terms, is a native of England, the 2nd in a family of 20 children.

Cook, William Hoff; son of Elisha Cook; was born at S. F., Nov. 29, 1859; graduated from Harvard College in 1880, with the degree of A. B.; qualified for the bar in Harvard Law School, 1881-82; was admitted to the bar of the California Supreme Court, Sept. 4, 1883.

Coolbrith, Miss Ina D.; favorite California authoress; for many years librarian of the Oakland Public Library; was complimented by the Bohemian Club with a delighful literary and musical entertainment, Sept. 1, 1893; a public sale of an album of sketches of California scenery contributed for her benefit, netted $1,025, April 21, 1875.

Coolidge, J. A.; well-known citizen; signed and verified the complaint filed in the Superior Court by order of the Board of Supervisors, to remove Mayor Kalloch from office, April 30, 1880.

Coon, Dr. H. P.; was Police Judge, 1856-60; Mayor, two terms, 1864-67; President Board of Heath, 1865-67.

Cooper, Dr. Elias S.; a celebrated physician and surgeon, and oculist, after whom "Cooper College" is named; was a native of Ohio; settled in S. F. in 1855; was one of the prime founders of the California State Medical Society; died of an extremely obscure and complicated nervous affection, Oct. 13, 1862, in his 40th year; (same age as Thos. Starr King;) his eventful professional career is sketched by his friend, Dr. Levi C. Lane, in "Representative Men of the Pacific"—with a poetic tribute by Thos. G. Spear.

Cooper, Mrs. Sarah B.; Christian philanthropist, devoted to Kindergarten work and Sabbath school teaching; was, with her daughter, Miss Hattie, asphyxiated by gas at her residence, 1902 Vallejo street, Dec, 11, 1896; it was the insane act of the daughter; Mrs. C. was born in N. Y., in 1834; her daughter in Tenn., in 1856; the funerals were from the First Congregational Church. Mrs. C. was a writer of book reviews and editorials in the Overland Monthly, from May, 1871 to May, 1874; for the ecclesiastical controversy between her and James B. Roberts—both of them leading members of Calvary Presbyterian Church—which resulted in their withdrawing to other churches, see Bulletin, Sept. 14, 15, 1881.

Cooper, Halsey F.; husband of Sarah B. Cooper, committed suicide, Dec. 6, 1885; a native of N. Y., aged 50; was alternately deputy collector of internal Revenue and Inspector of Customs, 1870-78; deputy surveyor of the port, 1879-85.

Cooper Medical College; the beautiful 5-story building, was publicly dedicated to the uses of medicine, Nov. 4, 1882; cost, $100,000; the gift of Dr. Levi C. Lane.

Cooper, Capt. John B. R.; pioneer of May, 1823; died Feb. 10, 1872, aged 79.

Cope, W. W.; distinguished jurist; Assemblyman from Amador, 1859; Justice of the Supreme Court, Sept. 20, 1859 to Jan. 2, 1864; Chief Justice, May 20, 1863 to Jan. 2, 1864; removed to S. F. in 1865; registered June 28, 1867, as a native of Kentucky, aged 44.

Copper Works, San Francisco; were established by Smith, Gowers & Neefus, 1851; Gowers, Neefus & Co., 1853; Gowers & Co., 1856.

Cora, Charles; his trial for the murder of U. S. Marshal Richardson, in front of where stands, in 1897, Campi's Restaurant, Clay street, was begun in Fourth District Court, Jan. 8, 1856, Judge John S. Hager, presiding; Col. E. D. Baker, counsel for the prisoner, was fined by Judge Hager for contempt, Feb. 28th. Sam White, Belle

SARAH B. COOPER.

Cora's financial agent, testified June 9th; the jury disagreeing, the great Vigilance Committee took Cora (and James P. Casey, who had killed James King of Wm.) from the County Jail, and publicly hung them, May 22, 1865. Belle Cora, a notorious woman of means, married Cora in the County Jail; she died in 1862, and her life was published in pamphlet.

Cora, Belle; wife of Chas. Cora; died Feb. 18, 1862; a native of Baltimore, Md., aged 35. See Casey and Cora.

Corbitt, William; owner of the San Mateo County Stock Farm, and of the celebrated trotting stallion, Guy Wilkes, was, from 1868 to 1891, senior partner of Corbitt & McCleay, wholesale grocers of Portland, Oregon, with office at S. F. His filly, Siva, by Guy Wilkes, won the trotting race at Detroit, Mich.; July 18, 1893, in 2:14½; 2:13¾; 2:16½, for the Merchants and Manufacturers' stake of $10,000. Guy Wilkes' daughter, Mary Best, won the trotting race at the Bay District Tract, S. F., July 2, 1893—time, 2:34; 2:31½, one mile. See Examiner, "More Glory for Guy Wilkes," July 27, 1893.

Cordage and Oakum Factory, The San Francisco; first in the State; was established by Flint, Peabody & Co. and Tubbs & Co., in 1856.

Cordell, Capt. Edward; of the U. S. Coast Survey; died suddenly on the street, Jan. 25, 1870.

Cormac, T. E. K.; who has been attorney for the British Consul at S. F. since his arrival in 1880; was one of the attorneys for Public Administrator Roach, 1883-87; born in the British Isles in 1844; a cadet in the Naval Academy near Trieste, and later a lieutenant in the Austro-Hungarian army; admitted to the bar in Boston, Mass.

Cornwall, P. B.; pioneer of Aug., 1848; was President of the Pioneers, 1865-66; and School Director, 1867-68; prominent and wealthy citizen; president of the Black Diamond Coal Mining Co., and of the Bellingham Bay and British Columbia R. R. Co.

Cornwall, Wm. A.; lawyer; Secretary State Senate, 1855; died Jan. 12, 1886; native of N. Y., aged 63.

Corporations; the first to organize in S. F., was the Ural Mining Company, which filed its articles, Aug. 26, 1851; the object was quartz mining in Nevada County; capital stock, $40,000, in 40 shares. Among the 12 directors were Judge Hager and William Norris.

Corson, J. G.; Assistant Engineer Fire Department; died at Vallejo, Feb. 8, 1871.

Cosmopolitan Hotel was opened Aug. 31, 1864; a great fire occurred in it April 23, 1867; damages, $150,000.

Cosmos Club was organized April, 1881; incorporated July, 1883.

Cotton, E. G.; manager of walking matches; committed suicide, on account of financial troubles, at Oakland, March 5, 1880; native of N. J., aged 33; his funeral was conducted by the Order of Elks.

Cowdery, J. F.; member of Assembly, 1873-74; and 1880; Speaker of the Assembly in 1880; City and County Attorney, 1882; registered June 24, 1867, as a native of N. Y., aged 32; for his controversy,

while City and County Attorney, with Supervisor Carmany, see
Bulletin, July 26, 1882, page 2.

Cowles, Samuel; Police Judge, 1861-63; County Judge, 1864-67; died Nov.
17, 1880, a native of Ohio, aged 57 years; funeral from Plymouth
Congregational Church.

Cox, Jerome B.; railroad contractor; killed the millionaire Chas. McLaugh-
lin, his whilom partner, in the latter's office, at S. F., Dec. 13, 1883.
Police Judge Lawlor discharged him on preliminary examination.
His long litigation with McL. is detailed in many volumes of the
Supreme Court Reports. For his suit against D. M. Delmas, see
local papers of July 22, 1893.

Cox, Hon. Samuel S.; ("Sunset Cox") M. C.; arrived overland July 18,
1871.

Craig, William; well-known lawyer; was City and County Attorney, Election Commissioner, and New City Hall Commissioner, 1883-84.

Crane, Henry F.; born in Vt., Jan. 31, 1833; admitted to the bar in St.
Lawrence County, N. Y., in 1860; located in S. F. in 1866; changed
his residence to Oakland in 1880; was a member of the State Land
Commission in 1876; in 1864 was Probate Judge of Boise County,
Idaho.

Crane, Lauren E.; journalist and expert accountant, committed suicide,
Feb. 16, 1897.

Crane, W. W., Jr.; a well-known S. F. lawyer; Senator from Alameda 1863-
64; his little story, "That Yankee Missionary," is in the Overland
Monthly for April, 1887.

Cranshaw, Richard; actor and author; committed suicide, May 1, 1864.

Craven, Mrs. Nettie R.; between whom and the heirs of the millionaire
James G. Fair, litigation opened in 1896, was born in Ohio; lived
in girlhood in Illinois and Iowa; came to California in 1874; taught
school in Oakland and Alameda for several years; then became a
teacher in the S. F. public schools; was elected Principal of the
Powell street school in 1879, and Principal of the Mission street
Grammar School in 1883. Author of a play entitled "Government
Claims," and is a contributor to magazines and educational journals.

A notice of Mrs. C., with a fine picture, is in an article on the
S. F. public schools, in the "Californian Magazine" for July, 1892,
page 292. And see Supplement at end of this volume.

Creigh, John D.; well-known citizen and lawyer; died June 4, 1882; a native of Penn., aged 85.

Cremation Company, (San Francisco) was incorporated Sept. 5, 1885.

Cremony, Capt. John C.; well-known citizen, attached to the C. H.; his life
and death are the subject of a sketch by Geo. E. Barnes, in Bulletin, Aug. 11, 1895.

Creswell, Harry T.; prominent lawyer; City and County Attorney, Election Commissioner, and City Hall Commissioner, for three terms,
1893-98; came to S. F. in 1870, from the State of Nevada, where he
was several times District Attorney, and once State Senator; was
born in Alabama, Dec. 10, 1850.

Cricket Match between officers of British frigate Zealous and the California Eleven, was won by the latter July 25, 1870.

Cricket, the Australian team arrived by sea, April 26, 1878.

Crittenden, Alex. P.; distinguished lawyer; was shot by Laura D. Fair, on the Oakland ferryboat, Nov. 3rd, and died Nov. 6, 1870; represented the Los Angeles district in the Assembly at the first session, 1849-50; and the Santa Clara district in the same body, 1852; his "mileage," for the first session, at 80 cents a mile, amounted to $1,136. Mr. C. was author of the time honored phrase in our statute, "The Common Law of England, so far as it is not repugnant to or inconsistent with the Constitution of the United States, or the Constitution or laws of the State of California, shall be the rule of decision in all the Courts of this State." This was his proposition in the Assembly, submitted April 4th, and became a law April 13, 1850.

Crocker, Charles; leading dry goods merchant of Sacramento in early years; represented Sacramento in the Assembly, 1861; one of the original incorporators of the Central Pacific Railroad Co., and the Southern Pacific Railroad Co.; married Miss Mary A. Deming at Sacramento, Nov. 27, 1852; their silver wedding was celebrated at S. F., 1000 persons present, Nov. 27, 1877; the papers of Nov. 28th contain his remarks on the occasion, detailing his career; sold out all of his holdings in all the railroad and steamship corporations to his associates in June, 1871; repurchased the same in Oct., 1873; removed from Sacramento to S. F. in 1875; drove the last spike in the California & Oregon railroad, at Ashland, Oregon, Dec. 17, 1887; President Southern Pacific R. R., 1876-85; changed his residence to N. Y. City in 1886, returning to S. F. in 1888; testified at N. Y. City before the Pacific R. R. Commission, Sept. 20, 1887; at a sale of paintings in N. Y., in Feb. 1888, Mr. C. paid $19,500, for Gerome's Serpent Charmer. He died at the Hotel del Monte, Monterey, Cal., Aug. 14, 1888; a native of Troy, N. Y., aged 65 years, 11 months. His estate was distributed by the Superior Court, S. F., Oct. 4, 1889, and amounted to $24,142,475. His will on file is to be found in the S. F. papers of Aug. 29, 1888. Sketch in Bancroft's "Contemporary Biography."

Crocker, Clark W.; brother of the preceding; of Sisson, Crocker & Co., railroad builders and contractors; died of a sudden stroke of paralysis at S. F., June 27, 1890, leaving a large estate; a native of N. Y., and came to California in 1850, to S. F. in 1875.

Crocker, H. S.; brother of the two preceding; a well-known stationer and early resident of Sacramento, opened the present large house of the H. S. Crocker Company in S. F., in 1871, John D. Yost being his partner. His brother, Charles Crocker, was a silent partner, putting $25,000 cash in the S. F. house.

Crocker, Mrs. Mary A.; widow of Charles Crocker, died at S. F., after a day's illness, in 1889.

Crocker, Miss Harriet; daughter of Charles and Mary A. Crocker, was married to Charles B. Alexander, a N. Y. City lawyer of wealth and prominence, at Grace Episcopal Church, S. F., at noon, April 26, 1887—the most brilliant nuptial event to occur in the city.

Crocker, Chas. F.; son of Charles Crocker; was born in Sacramento, Cal., Dec. 26, 1854; was educated in the public schools of that city, and in the Polytechnic Institute of Brooklyn, N. Y.; removed from Sacramento to S. F. in 1878, and took a position as clerk of the Central Pacific R. R. Co., being stationed on the Oakland wharf; the next year he became Vice President of the Southern Pacific R. R. Co.; so continued till 1885, when he became 3rd Vice President of that Co.; held latter office to 1887; 2nd Vice President same company, 1887-90; Vice President 1890-97; President Southern Pacific R. R. Co., of Arizona, 1881-86; President Market Street Railway Co., 1893-97; a Regent of the University of California, appointed by Gov. Waterman, March, 1, 1888; term will expire in 1904; one of the original 24 trustees of the Leland Stanford, Jr., University, appointed in Nov., 1885; one of the executors of his father's will; bore the expense of the "Eclipse of the Sun" expedition to South America, Dec. 27, 1889; presented the Native Sons of the Golden West with $10,000 to purchase "Sutter's Fort," Sacramento, Dec., 1889; married Miss Jennie M., daughter of Ansel I. Easton, Sept., 1880; served upon the staff of Gov. Perkins, with rank of Colonel, 1880-82; was presented by his father with the elegant residence, S. W. corner Pine and Leavenworth streets, (lot 137½x185), Sept. 6, 1880.

Crocker, Wm. H.; brother of the preceding, has been President of the Crocker-Woolworth Bank since 1893, and from the incorporation of the bank to that time was cashier thereof.

Crocker's San Francisco Directory, published by the H. S. Crocker Company, first appeared in and for the year 1895.

Crocker-Langley Directory appeared in and for the year 1896—by the H. S. Crocker Company, which had recently purchased from Painter & Co., Langley's Directory and merged it with their own. Langley's Directory had been issued annually since 1858, in which year it was established by Henry G. Langley. See Langley, Henry G.

Crocker, Mrs. Jennie M.; wife of Col. Chas. F. Crocker, and daughter of Ansel I. Easton, married, Sept., 1880, died at S. F., March 25, 1887, aged 28.

Crocker, Chas. W.; editor and proprietor of the "Craftsman," died Aug. 2, 1876; native of Ohio, aged 45.

Crocker-Woolworth National Bank was organized Aug. 31, 1886.

Crokett, J. B.; distinguished jurist; Judge of the Supreme Court from Dec., 1867 to Jan. 5, 1880; died at Fruitvale, Jan. 15, 1884.

Cronise, Wm. H. V ; pioneer of June 4, 1849; donated $1,000 to benevolent societies, Jan. 1, 1872.

Crook, Gen.; redoubtable Indian fighter; was banqueted by prominent citizens, April 12, 1875.

Cross Country Club was organized Jan. 15, 1890.

Crowley, Patrick; Constable, First Township, 1858-65; Chief of Police, 1866-73; and Chief of Police and one of the Police Commissioners since 1880; is still in office; registered Aug. 4, 1866, as a native of N. Y., aged 35; when going out of office for a short time as Chief of Police, he was presented with a magnificent gold watch and chain by police officers, Dec. 1, 1873.

Cruelty to Children, Society for the Prevention of, was incorporated Sept. 2, 1876.

Culver, J. H.; Member of Assembly, 1883; School Director, 1882; 1885-86; 1891-94; registered June 18, 1866, as a native of N. Y., aged 40.

Cummins, Adley H.; philologist and lawyer, was a native of Penn., came to California in 1869, at the age of 19, and died of heart disease at 39. There is a sketch of his life in "The Story of the Files."

Cummins, Ella Sterling; widow of the preceding; author of "The Story of the Files: a Review of Californian Writers and Literature;" octavo, 437 pages; issued under the auspices of the World's Fair Commission of California, 1893. Her first novel, "Little Mountain Princess," appeared in 1880. She was born in Sacramento, Cal. Mrs. D. H. Haskell, of S. F., is her mother. "The Story of the Files" had run through The Wasp, for six months, in 1891, under the title, "Library of Californian Writers."

Cunningham, Lewis; pioneer of Sept. 26, 1849; State Senator from Yuba, 1863-66; early banker at Marysville; Harbor Commissioner at S. F., 1873-74; died Oct. 25, 1879; native of N. Y. City, aged 68; funeral from Calvery Presbyterian Church; his estate was appraised, Feb. 25, 1880, at $255,810.

Cunningham, Rev. Thos. M., D. D.; long pastor of the First Presbyterian Church, and later of the Central Tabernacle, died at Oakland, Feb. 22, 1880.

Curious Case; in a contest over the large estate of an almost stillborn child, Judge Blake held that there was life in the child when born, and appointed the mother as administratrix, Sept. 23, 1863. (Estate of Joseph M. Garwood.)

Currey, John; bar leader and distinguished jurist; a pioneer of Aug. 18, 1849; was born in Westchester County, N. Y., in Oct., 1814; Justice of the Supreme Court for four years ending Jan. 1, 1868; Chief Justice, 1866-67; after his retirement from the bench, he formed a partnership with Oliver P. Evans, which continued for eight years, until Jan. 1, 1878, when he withdrew from practice on account of failing eyesight. A chapter of "Bench and Bar in California" is devoted to his life.

Curry, C. F.; Member of Assembly, 1887; County Clerk, 1895-98.

Curtis, J. F.; who was Chief of Police, in 1856-57, is now and for many years has been a prominent resident of Idaho.

Custom House Grounds; west side of Battery street, extending from Washington to Jackson. The U. S Government purchased this property of the State of California, for $150,000, Sept. 7, 1854. R. P. Hammond, Collector of the Port, "to save to the United States a large sum of money," proposed to pay the amount in California State bonds, but Gov. Bigler would not accept the bonds, and payment was made in coin. (Senate Journal, 1855, pages 70-71.)

Cutler, E. B.; well-known lawyer; was the Republican candidate for State Senator, 9th district, in 1882, and candidate of the same party for Police Judge in 1886. He is a graduate of Columbian College, Washington, D. C., Hastings College of the Law, and of the University of California, and was admitted to the bar of the California Supreme Court in May, 1882. Was born in Ohio, June 27, 1836.

Cutter, James H.; prominent commission merchant, 1855-61; wholesale grocer, 1861-68; Treasurer Fire Department Charitable Fund, 1862-69; State Harbor Commissioner, Dec., 1867 to June 12, 1870, when he died.

Czapkay, Dr. L. J.; well-known physician; removed after a long practice in S. F., to Portland, Oregon, where he died, May 27, 1882. He built and owned for some years the four-story brick building on Washington street, adjoining the old City Hall, long known by his name.

D

Dahl. Christian J.; a lawyer who was raised to the trade of a machinist, was master of S. F. lodge No. 68, International Association of Machinists, before removing to Los Angeles in 1892. He was born in Iowa, April 10, 1865; and was admitted to the bar at S. F., July 20, 1891.

Daingerfield, Wm. P.; a widely known jurist, settled in S. F., in 1865; was Judge of the 12th District Court, 1876-79; Presiding Judge of the Superior Court, in 1880; expired suddenly while holding Court, four months after taking office, May 5, 1880; had been Judge of the 9th District Court at Shasta before locating in S. F. A sketch of his career is in the Evening Post, of Jan. 20, 1883. Was a native of Virginia.

Daingerfield, Wm. R.; son of the preceding; was elected in Nov., 1892, Judge of the Superior Court for the unexpired term ending Dec. 31, 1894, and was elected in Nov., 1894, for six years from Jan., 1895; was born at Shasta, Cal., June 9, 1857; is a graduate of the University of California, and was admitted to the bar of the Supreme Court in Oct., 1879.

Dairymen's Union of California opened business in 1892 at 113-119 Davis

street, which is the present location. Wm. S. Pierce was president,
Wm. Hatton, secretary, and Louis Tomasini, manager. Henry
Brunner became secretary in 1894, succeeded by John R. Denman
in 1895; in 1895, also, Warren Dutton became president, Geo. W.
Burbank, vice president, and E. W. Steele, treasurer; Mr. Tomasini
continues as manager.

Dake, Edmund C.; who had been a leading clothing merchant since 1858,
established Dake's Advertising Agency, in 1882, and is still con-
ducting it as sole proprietor; his son Edmund D. Dake, being manager.

Dall, Capt. C. C.; veteran captain of ocean steamers, died June 14, 1885; a
native of N. Y., aged 54.

Dall, W. H.; his lines on the Death of Louis Agassiz, appeared in 1873, and
are in "California Anthology."

Dalliba, Henry S.; veteran newspaper reporter, in continuous service in
that sphere longer than any other man in the State, came to S. F.,
in 1850; was bookkeeper on the Evening Journal, 1856; was one of
those who hastened to the help of James King of Wm., editor of
the Bulletin, when that hero was shot down by Casey, May 14, 1856,
and carried him into the Pacific Express office; was bookkeeper
of the Herald, 1860-61; was local reporter on Bulletin for 23 years
before his death, which occurred at S. F., Dec. 14, 1896; Mr. D.
was a native of Mass., aged 61, and was buried from St. Mary's
Cathedral.

Dalton, Frank; a leading produce commission merchant since 1871; was a
School Director, in 1889-90, and President of the Board of Education during his term of two years.

Daly, Patrick Henry; died Dec. 10, 1867, holding the office of Fire Commissioner, and while Supervisor for the Third Ward, aged 97 years.

Dameron, James P.; well-known lawyer, and owner of valuable real property in the city and other parts of the State, registered on June 2,
1866, as a native of N. C., aged 36. He came to California at a very
early day, and for a few years delved in the mines of Placer Co.
A notice of his life is in the Post, of June 16, 1882.

D'Ancona, A. A.; physician, and professor of physiology in the medical
and dental departments of the State University, has been in medical practice at S. F. since 1886, before which he was a teacher in
the public schools for six years.

D'Ancona, Alex. D.; a graduate of the University of California; located in
S. F., in 1870; taught in the public schools, 1876-80; was admitted
to the bar of the State Supreme Court, May 30, 1881. He was born
in N. Y., Nov. 2, 1855.

Danforth, Edwin; prominent citizen, who was a member of the Board of
Supervisors for the years 1878-79; was bookkeeper of the Broadway
Bonded Warehouse, 1871-74; from 1874 to 1894 he was sole pro-
prietor of that property; since 1894, Mr. Edward P. Danforth and
Mr. Chas. H. Gilman have been associated with him. Mr. D. reg-
istered Sept. 6., 1870, as a native of Mass., aged 41

Daniels, Joseph; for many years bookkeeper of the S. F. Gas Light Co., died May 25, 1886; a native of Mass., aged 76. Sketch written by direction of Mr. Geo. K. Fitch, is in Bulletin of May 26, 1886.

Danish Society (Norden) was organized in July, 1873.

Danziger, Dr. Gustav Adolf; a student of Semitic literature, and joint author with Ambrose Bierce of the novel, "The Monk and the Hangman's Daughter," was a practicing dentist in S. F., 1888-94. He was born in Austria; came to America in boyhood, and to California, in 1887.

Dartmouth College Alumni Association was organized in 1881.

Darwin, Chas. Ben.; prominent lawyer, is a pioneer of Sept., 1849; was Assistant District Attorney, 1872-73; 1876-77; 1878-79; is a native of N. Y., and was admitted to the bar in Tenn., in 1848; was distinguished at the bar and in legislation in Tennessee and Iowa before coming to this State.

Dashaway Association opened their new hall, on Post street, Nov. 3, 1878.

Daughters of the American Revolution; Sequoia Chapter was organized Dec. 10, 1891.

Davidson, George; eminent engineer; was Assistant in the U. S. Coast Survey at S. F., from 1869 to 1895; was born in England, in May, 1825; was made a citizen in Philadelphia, in Nov., 1848; is author of many historical and scientific works and papers. Prof. D. was invited by a unanimous vote of the Board of Supervisors, passed Oct. 26, 1885, to present his views upon the sewerage system of S. F.; his report, dated April 15, 1886, was read in the Board, May 3, 1886, and was, by order of the Board, published in pamphlet form. It is found in Municipal Reports for 1885-86, pages 107-114 of appendix. The Professor took passage, with a party, on the steamer for Japan, Aug. 29, 1874, to observe the transit of Venus. He was appointed by Gov. Irwin, regent of the State University, Dec. 17, 1879, vice John B. Felton, deceased; was President of the California Academy of Natural Sciences, 1881-83; a sketch of his life is in Bancroft's "Contemporary Biography."

Davidson, B., & Co.; bankers, were established in 1849; Mr. D., who was a pioneer of Aug. 18, 1849, died at Sidmouth, Devonshire, England, Sept. 21, 1878, after a long illness, aged 56. A copy of his will was filed for probate in S. F., June 1, 1880; his estate in England was worth $500,000, besides a fine park in Devonshire; his estate in California was appraised at $101,000.

Davidson, William W.; well-known lawyer; was born in Mo., Sept. 4, 1857; received the degree of A. B. from the California College in 1878; graduated from Hastings College in the class of 1882; in May of that year was admitted to the bar of the State Supreme Court; located in S. F., in May, 1883.

Davidson, J. W., & Co.; (John W. Davidson, Wm. Davidson, Geo. H. Huntsman, and Raphael and Henry Weill) large wholesale and retail fancy and domestic dry goods house, was established by J. W. Davidson and R. Lane (D. & L.), in 1854; the style became J. W.

GUSTAV ADOLF DANZIGER.

Davidson & Co., when Raphael Weill took Mr. Lane's interest in 1857; Mr. Huntsman entered in 1862; Wm. Davidson and Henry Weill, in 1868; the partners, in 1881, were J. W. Davidson and Raphael and Henry Weill, and so continued to 1885, when the style became as at present, Raphael Weill & Co., the partners being Raphael and Henry Weill and Eugene Gallois. Albert Roullier became a member of the firm in 1889; the firm since 1892, has been composed of Raphael Weill, Eugene Gallois, and Albert Roullier. The house was incorporated in 1895, as Raphael Weill & Co., with Mr. Weill as president, Mr. Gallois, first vice president, Mr. Roullier, second vice president, and Alexander Hamilton, secretary.

Davidson Observatory, U. S. Coast and Geodetic Survey, Astronomical and Telegraph Longitude Station, was established by Prof. Geo. Davidson in 1884, in Lafayette Park, corner Octavia and Clay streets, where it still stands.

Davidson & Leigh, (Geo. Davidson and E. A. Leigh) the prominent real estate and insurance house, was established in 1890; both gentlemen had been together for many years up to that time with O. Livermore, the large real estate owner and dealer, to whose business they succeeded.

Davis, A. Mc. F.; was a School Director for the years 1874-75; and was President of the Board of Education, in 1875.

Davis, Horace; distinguished citizen and scholar; was born in Mass., in 1831; his father John Davis, was Gov. of Mass., 1841-45, and afterwards for ten years a Member of the National House of Representatives, and for sixteen years U. S. Senator. Horace Davis graduated from Harvard College in 1849; arrived at S. F. around the Horn, April 1, 1853; established the Golden Gate Flouring Mills, in 1860; was a Member of the National House of Representatives, for two terms, March 4, 1877-March 4, 1881; married Miss Edith, daughter of Thos. Starr King, in Feb., 1875. Mr. Davis was President of the Mercantile Library Association, 1864; President of the Produce Exchange, 1866-76; President of the Chamber of Commerce, 1883-84. He was one of the original trustees of the Leland Stanford, Jr. University, named in the grant of Nov. 11, 1885. He was inaugurated President of the University of California, March 23, 1888. He is the author of an essay on Shakespeare's Sonnets, in Overland Monthly, 1887, which was reprinted in pamphlet; bought the home of Henry A. Palmer at Berkeley for $20,000, May, 1888. Sketch and portrait of Mr. D. are in "Resources of California," Sept., 1886.

Davis, Henry L.; a prominent citizen who was Sheriff for two terms, 1864-67; was born in R. I., Oct. 17, 1827; was one of the organizers of the California Wire Works, and of the cable system of street railways; has been the head of the California Optical Co. since 1888. He removed his residence to N. Y. in 1883, and returned to S. F. in May, 1888.

Davis, John W.; a discharged U. S. soldier, committed suicide May 1, 1871, and was buried as a pauper. Twenty years later it was discovered that he had a "nest egg" in a savings bank, which had grown to over $1,000. No heir can be found.

Davis, Jacob Z.; millionaire, and pioneer of Aug. 4, 1849; a valuable friend of the Mining Bureau and of the Societies for prevention of cruelty; died Oct. 28, 1896, while visiting at Philadelphia; his remains were cremated, pursuant to his wish.

Dawsey, Mrs. Sarah; (colored;) died Nov. 6, 1870, aged 113 years.

Day, Thomas, & Co.; importers and manufacturers of gas and electric fixtures, was incorporated in 1886. This house was established by Thomas Day, who was an oil and camphine chandler at No. 732 Montgomery street, near Jackson (old No. 188) as early as 1855; he very soon imported gas fixtures, and otherwise enlarged his business, and in 1869, opened an additional and more stylish store at 335 Pine street; the old Montgomery street place was closed in 1874; from 1876 to 1886, the business was at 122-124 Sutter street; was removed to its present location, 222 Sutter, at the time of incorporation, in 1886. From 1883 to the present, the business has been owned by Frank J. Symmes and Vanderlynn Stow, and ever since the incorporation, Mr. Symmes has been president, and Mr. Stow, secretary and treasurer.

Dean, James O.; was Auditor of the Savings and Loan Society, 1863-73; License Collector, Sept. 14, 1874-Dec. 31, 1875.

Dean, Peter; President of the Merchants' Exchange Bank of S. F., since 1883, is a pioneer of June 10, 1849; was President of the Pioneers, July, 1877-July, 1878; was State Senator, 1877-78; registered on June 6, 1870, as a native of England, aged 41.

Deane, Dr. Charles Tennyson; distinguished physician and surgeon; has practiced in S. F., since 1865; was a School Director in 1885-86. He registered on June 1, 1866, as a native of N. Y., aged 27.

Deane, John; of Murphy, Grant & Co., died at his residence, Claremont, Alameda Co., April 27, 1885; a native of Ireland, aged 52 years, 7 months; was buried with the rites of the Catholic Church; a brother of Coll and Hugh E. Deane.

Deal, W E. F.; a prominent lawyer; born in Md., March 8, 1840; graduated from Dickinson College (Penn.), 1859; arrived in S. F. in the same year; taught school at Oakland, in 1859-60; and at Colusa a part of 1860; and at Nevada City, 1861-63; was admitted to the bar of the Supreme Court of the State of Nevada, in 1865, and of the U. S. Supreme Court at Washington, D. C., in 1876; settled in S. F., in 1894.

Deck, Auguste; died in Oct., 1853, leaving an estate of $100,000; efforts to escheat the property failed. For "The Great Deck Case," see Bulletin, Aug. 9, 10, 1856, and Oct. 10, 1859; Supreme Court Reports, vol. 6, page 666, and vol. 12, page 433; also Senate Journal, 5th session, page 447.

De Fremery, Jas. & Co.; importers and commission merchants; James de

Fremery who is still the head of this house, was in the business as early as 1855; his partner, Wm. C. B. de Fremery, joined him in 1868, when the present style of the house was assumed. Mr. James de Fremery was consul for Mecklenburg-Schwerin from 1859 to 1869; consul for the Netherlands, 1863 to 1891; President of the S. F. Savings Union, 1868-82; and his firm were agents for the Amsterdam Board of Underwriters from 1870 to 1891. During this long period, both partners have always resided in Oakland.

De Haro Title; settlers on the Potrero fired 200 guns, on receipt of news that the U. S. Supreme Court had decided against the De Haro claimants, May 14, 1867.

Francisco De Haro died Jan. 1, 1849, leaving no will; for his estate and heirs, see Mahoney vs. Middleton, 41 Cal., 43; for interesting early history, see Sill vs. Reese, 47 Cal., 296.

De Haven, John J.; distinguished lawyer and jurist, upon leaving the bench of the Supreme Court, in Jan., 1895, located in S. F., and formed a law partnership with S. C. Denson, once Superior Judge of Sacramento Co., which partnership continues (Denson & De Haven). Judge De Haven's previous residence was in Humboldt Co., which he represented in the Assembly, Dec. 6, 1869 to April 4, 1870. He was one of 12 Republicans in a body of 80 members, and towards the middle of the session was added to the judiciary committee, on motion of the Chairman, Naphtaly, Democrat. He was also Senator from Humboldt at the sessions of 1871-72 and 1873-74. His term of service on the Supreme Bench was four years.

Delmas, D. M.; distinguished lawyer, was born in France, of French parents, April 14, 1844; son of a California pioneer of 1849, he followed the latter in 1854, and graduated from Santa Clara College in 1863, receiving, with the highest honors, the degree of Master of Arts; graduated from the Law Department of Yale College, 1865; admitted to the bar of the Supreme Court of Connecticut, Sept., 1865, and of the Supreme Court of California, in Feb., 1866; was District Attorney, Santa Clara Co., 1868-69. Mr. D. removed to S. F. in 1882. When the Democratic State Convention, at Stockton, declared against Judge Field's presidential aspirations, in 1884, Mr. D. led the anti-Field majority. He bought the family residence of Wm. T. Coleman, S. W. corner Taylor and Washington streets, for $40,000, in 1890; while he was a Regent of the University of California, he was President of the Day at the inauguration of Hon. Horace Davis as President of the University, March 23, 1888; formed a law partnership with Samuel M. Shortridge, in 1893, which still continues.

Delabigne, J. B.; old flour merchant; committed suicide Oct. 3, 1867, aged 75.

Delany, Chas. McC.; was City Attorney, Jan.-Nov., 1852; died near Napa City, May 26, 1881, a native of Ireland, aged 55.

De Lesseps, Ferdinand; distinguished French engineer, who built the

Suez Canal, arrived March 17, 1880; he was then 75 years old, and visiting the U. S. in the interest of the Panama Canal.

Demokrat, California; German daily morning paper, now the oldest daily existing on the Pacific coast, was founded in 1853, by Dr. F. Von Loehr; it was bought by its present owner, Mr. Frederick Hess, in 1858, he then being only eighteen years of age.

Demorest, Dr. Jacob M.; committed suicide with poison, Dec. 30, 1877.

Denio, Walter S.; melter and refiner at the U. S. Mint, died of congestion of the lungs, Feb. 10, 1865, aged 36.

Denman, James; influential citizen; was principal of the Denman public school, (now a grammar school for girls) from Nov. 17, 1851 to June, 1857; and from July 3, 1864, to Dec., 1867; and from Jan., 1871 to Dec., 1873; and from June 13, 1876 to 1889, when he permanently retired. Mr. D. was Superintendent of Common Schools, 1859-61; 1868-70; and 1874-75; and a member of the Board of Education, Oct. 9, 1889 to Jan., 1891; and a member of the Board of Supervisors, 1893-94. For his valuable historical sketch of the Public Schools of S. F., including the Denman Medal Fund, see Municipal Reports, 1879-80, page 632. Mr. D. registered on June 5, 1866, as a native of N. Y., aged 37. A sketch of his life is in Bancroft's "Contemporary Biography."

Denman Medal Fund for Girls; was established by James Denman in June, 1865, by a donation of $1,000, the interest of which was to be expended annually in procuring silver medals for the most deserving pupils of the Denman Grammar School.

Denman Grammar School Building, N. W. Bush and Taylor streets, was completed and opened in 1864. James Denman was the first principal of this school, (in 1851) which was given his name upon his first retirement from teaching, on account of ill health, in 1857. He was also the first principal of the school, after the erection of the present building, in 1864.

Dennison, F. S.; lieutenant U. S. Navy; committed suicide on April 18, 1873.

Denny, G. J.; a marine painter, of S. F., of some distinction, died suddenly at Cambria, San Luis Obispo Co., Oct. 7, 1886. Irving M. Scott has one of his best pictures. The large marine view in the office of the Lick House is by him; also were the drop curtains of the old Academy of Music and Maguire's Opera House. He was born in Delaware, and reached the age of 50 years.

Denson, S. C.; prominent lawyer; was born in Illinois, Sept. 23, 1839; arrived in California in 1860; admitted to the bar of the Supreme Court of Nevada Territory in March, 1864; was Assemblyman from Ormsby Co., Nev., 1864-65; District Attorney, same county, 1866-68; resigned, and located in Sacramento, Cal., in 1868; was District Judge for Sacramento and Yolo, 1876-79; first Superior Judge of Sacramento under the Constitution of 1879; presided at the celebrated trial of Troy Dye, for the murder of A. M. Tullis; removed to S. F. in 1889.

Desmond, Thomas; was Sheriff in 1880-81; elected by the Workingmen's Party.

Desty, Robert; an industrious writer of law books; was principal of the West End School, 1867-68; elected joint Senator for S. F. and San Mateo, on the Workingmen's ticket, 1879; was refused his seat by the Republican majority, on the ground that his naturalization was defective; he removed to Rochester, N. Y., in 1880, continuing his law writings, and died there in 1896; was a native of Canada. His true full name was Robert Daillibout d'Estimanville de Beau Mouchi.

Deuprey, Eugene N.; prominent lawyer; was born in Louisiana, in 1850; grew up from early boyhood, in S. F.; pursued his law studies in the office of the noted firm of the Shafters; came to the bar in 1871, and very soon took a commanding place.

Deutscher Krieger Verein was organized in 1884.

Deveny, Peter; a Member of the Assembly, in 1885; School Director, 1881, appointed March 14, 1881, vice N. B. Stone, resigned; was Clerk Justices Court, 1886-88; Fee Clerk, Treasurer's office, since 1895.

Devine, John; "The Chicken;" was executed for the murder of August Kamp, May 14, 1873.

Devine, P. J.; a prominent sculptor, died Jan. 1, 1870.

Devoto, James Augustus; was born at S. F., July 29, 1869; educated at the S. F Grammar and High Schools; graduated from Hastings Law College and took a further course of study in Rome; was admitted to the bar of the California Supreme Court, May 5, 1890.

Dewey & Co.; (Geo. H. Strong, A. T. Dewey, and W. B. Ewer) patent solicitors; and the Dewey Publishing Co., J. F. Halloran, general manager, publishers of the Pacific Rural Press, and the Mining and Scientific Press, had a common origin in the firm of Ewer & Smith (Warren B. Ewer and C. W. M. Smith) who established the last named paper in 1863. Mr. A. T. Dewey entered the firm the next year, when it was styled Dewey & Co., and the business of patent agents was added. Mr. Smith withdrew, and Geo. H. Strong and Jno. L. Boone entered, in 1870, when the firm began the Pacific Rural Press. The firm added "wood engraving" to their business in 1873; Gen. Boone withdrew, and "photo engraving" was added to the business in 1879. Both the firm and business were divided in 1880, when there became two firms of the name of Dewey & Co., one composed of Alfred T. Dewey and Warren B. Ewer, the other of Alfred T. Dewey, Warren B. Ewer, and Geo. H. Strong; the first named continued the publication of the papers already mentioned and also began the publication of the Pacific States Watchman, a weekly, devoted to fraternal orders; they also continued the engraving business; the other firm held to patent agencies; the publishing firm took the style of the Dewey Publishing Co., in 1892, with Alfred Holman as manager, succeeded by Mr. Halloran the next year.

Dewey, Squire P.; pioneer of July 5, 1849; acquired large wealth in real

estate; returned to N. Y., his native State, in 1885; contributed
$250 to the Starr King Monument in June, 1888; contributed $500
to the Bush Relief Fund for laborers, March 3, 1880; died in N. Y.
City, in April, 1889, at the age of 70; a sketch is in Bancroft's
"Contemporary Biography;" for his litigation with Rodman M.
Price, see Chapter on John T. Doyle in " Bench and Bar." He was
tried on charge of criminal libel of Rodman M. Price, and was acquitted, Nov. 17, 1880.

Dewing Company, The J.; publishers; and importers and manufacturers
of pianos; Jas. Dewing, president; Madison S. Dewing, vice president; this firm has had this style since 1886; from that year
back to 1883, it was in two parts, both styled J. Dewing & Co.; one,
composed of James and Madison S. Dewing, carried on the
business of publishers and booksellers; the other (James, Madison
S. and Amasa J. Dewing) that of piano makers; except that Jas.
Dewing had no partner in the publishing business in the years
1883-84-85.

This now reorganized house had its foundation in that of
Dewing & Laws (Francis Dewing and Jeremiah Laws) importers
of subscription books, established in 1864. This latter became
Francis Dewing & Co., in 1867; Mr. James Dewing, the present
president, became a partner in 1871.

Dey, Richard V.; capitalist; was executor, with John W. Mackay, of the
will of Mrs. Theresa Fair; their final account as such executors
was settled July 13, 1893; their commissions amounted to $52,786,
on an estate of $5,096,646; Mr, Dey was presented by John W.
Mackay, with a gold watch costing $500, at Virginia City, Nev.,
July 6, 1881.

De Young, Charles; senior proprietor and founder of the Chronicle, shot
and dangerously wounded Isaac S. Kalloch, on Aug. 23, 1879. K.
was then running for Mayor on the Workingmen's ticket, and was
elected while confined in bed from his injuries. Mr. De Young
was shot and killed by Isaac M. Kalloch on April 23, 1880. He was
a native of Louisiana, aged 35. His brain was found to weigh 44
ounces.

De Young, M. H.; one of the founders, and, since the death of his brother
in 1880, sole proprietor of the San Francisco Chronicle, was shot and
dangerously wounded by A. B. Spreckels on Nov. 19, 1884. S. was
acquitted by a jury in the Superior Court. Mr. D. was Director
General of the Midwinter Fair of 1893; he gave $5,000 to that en-
terprise on July 13, 1893; he registered Oct. 1, 1867, as a native of
Missouri, aged 21. " Benefits of the Midwinter Exposition, S. F.",
an article by M. H. De Young, appeared in the Californian
Magazine for March, 1894. At the election of U. S. Senator in the
legislature, Jan. 22, 1895, among the candidates placed in nomina-
tion, Mr. D. received 4 votes in the Senate, and 12 in the Assembly.
This was the occasion when Hon. Geo. C. Perkins was first elected,
for the unexpired term of Senator Stanford.

M. H. de YOUNG.

Mrs. M. H. De Young pressed the electric button which set in motion the machinery at Sunset City, Jan. 27, 1894 (California Midwinter Exposition at S. F.).

Diamond, Miss Carrie; an attractive young woman, doing a large business as a milliner at 402 Kearny street, died suddenly under suspicious circumstances, on Nov. 28, 1869. A well-known citizen was indicted for her murder, and was tried and acquitted. Dr. Isaac Rowell testified that she died from a clot of blood on the brain.

Diamond. G. E. D.; a book canvasser, who had located in S. F. some seven years prior, completed his 100th year, May 1, 1896; is still living at this publication.

Dibble, Henry C. prominent lawyer, editorial writer and politician; was born in Indiana, Nov. 8, 1844; received an academic education, and graduated from the Law School of Louisiana State University; admitted to the bar in New Orleans, June 20, 1865; was Judge of the Eighth District Court in that city, and Assistant Attorney General of Louisiana; located in S. F. in Feb., 1883; in 1885-86, he was Assistant U. S. Attorney at S. F., under Hon. S. G. Hilborn; was Assemblyman from S. F. in 1889, 1891, 1897.

Dickens Ball; in aid of the S. F. Female Hospital, was held at Union Hall, April 16, 1874.

Dickinson, John H.; prominent lawyer; State Senator, from S. F., 1880-81, State Senator from Marin and Contra Costa, 1897-99; was Colonel of the First Regiment, N. G. C., for eight years ending in 1891; Brig.-Gen'l, by appointment of Gov. Markham, 1891-94; was born in Virginia, April 8, 1849; admitted to the bar of the Supreme Court of California, in April, 1873, and has since followed the profession in S. F. Established his residence in Sausalito, Marin Co., in 1893.

Dietrich, Wm. K.; who was County Recorder for the years 1880-81, was a dealer in meats in the principal markets from the Fifties down to to 1874; manager of the S. F. Packing and Provision Co., in 1874-75; U. S. Meat Inspector, 1877-78; Cashier in the Tax Collector's office, 1885-86; and has been a dealer in real estate since 1888, residing in Berkeley.

Dime Savings Bank, Cosmopolitan, failed on Dec. 18, 1877.

Dimond, Gen. Wm. H.; prominent citizen; was Park Commissioner, 1887-89; Superintendent U. S. Mint, under President Harrison, 1890-93; Gen. Dimond was born of American missionary parents in the Sandwich Islands; he died in 1896; estate was appraised Nov. 18, 1896, at $125,804, of which his ⅓ interest in the house of Williams, Dimond & Co., was valued at $26,000.

Mrs. Dimond died at S. F., Jan. 15, 1890; a notice of her, with with references to the General, is in Bulletin of Jan. 16th.

Diphtheria became epidemic in S. F., in the closing days of Nov., 1876.

Directory of San Francisco; the first was issued by Chas. P. Kimball, Sept., 1850; it was a 12-mo. of 136 pages, and contained 2500 names. "See Crocker-Langley Directory."

Dividend Building on the westerly corner of Pine and Leidesdorff streets, was begun in 1877, and completed in 1878.

"Dive Ordinance;" was held to be unconstitutional by Superior Judge Wm. P. Daingerfield and seven of his associates, Feb. 18, 1880; Judges John Hunt and J. F. Sullivan disented, in an opinion published in the Bulletin, Feb. 20, 1880.

Dixon, Wm. Hepworth; distinguished English author and lecturer, visited S. F. in Dec., 1874; he delivered a lecture on the "German Empire," on Dec. 15, 1874.

Doble, Abner; prominent citizen; head of the Abner Doble Co., electrical and mechanical engineers, importers and manufacturers of iron and steel; began his long business career in S. F., as a blacksmith. He was with Thos. Nelson (N. & D., blacksmiths), 1855 to 1878; in 1878, succeeded to Nelson & Doble in their horse shoeing business and in the manufacture of cast steel tools, also in the agency for Thos. Firth & Sons, Sheffield, England; became president of the Abner Doble Co. on its organization in 1889; which company still holds the agency for Firth & Sons, for various important iron and steel inventions. Mr. D. was a member of the Board of Education, from July 19, 1864, to the end of 1865; in 1869-79 he was vice president of the Fulton Iron Works. On the 15th of March, 1897, Mr. D. was struck by a railroad locomotive at Berkeley, and was seriously injured.

Doane, Chas.; who was Sheriff for five years, (1857-61) died suddenly, of apoplexy, Oct. 7, 1862.

Doane, Micah; of Doane & Co., well-known drayman, was a member of the Board of Supervisors, 1880-81. Mr. D. was a manufacturer of hay presses in 1862; he has been in his present business since 1863; the present firm was formed in 1880.

Dodge, Henry L.; distinguished citizen; a pioneer of May 1, 1849; was secretary of the two Town Councils immediately before the city's incorporation, Aug. 6, 1849, to May 8, 1850; was a Supervisor in 1861-62; Assemblyman, 1863; State Senator, 1863-64, and 1865-66; President of the Pioneers, 1879-80; Superintendent of the U. S. Mint, from Dec., 1877, to June 18, 1881; President of the Board of Education, 1895-96. Mr. D. prepared for the bar at Burlington, Vt., and practiced law in S. F from 1850 to 1854. He is one of the original trustees of Leland Stanford, Jr., University, named in the grant of Nov. 11, 1885; he first registered as a voter on June 7, 1866, as a native of Vt., aged 41. See Dodge, Sweeney & Co.

Dodge, Sweeney & Co. (Henry L. Dodge, Lorenzo H. Sweeney, John E. Ruggles, and F. W. Van Sicklen), wholesale provision and commission merchants; this firm was formed in 1876 by the three gentlemen first named, at 406 Front street. Messrs. Sweeney and Ruggles had been associated with John Sroufe in the same business, at the same place for five years, under the style of Sroufe, Sweeney & Co.; prior to that period, for some years, Mr. Dodge and Mr. Sroufe had conducted the business, as Dodge & Sroufe, at the same place. The present firm has had its large store at 114-116 Market street, running through to 11-13 California street, since 1881, in which year Mr. Van Sicklen became a partner.

Dominican Fathers, Church of, corner Bush and Steiner streets, was dedicated, June 29, 1873.

Donahue, James; brother of Peter Donahue; pioneer of April 24, 1849; died at his country residence near Santa Clara, Aug. 17, 1862.

Donahue, Jas. Mervyn; son of Peter Donahue, and son-in-law of Hon. Wm. T. Wallace, was President of the S. F. & North Pacific Coast R. R., 1887, to March 3, 1890, when he died at S. F., the place of his birth, aged 30 years and 10 months.

Donahue, Peter; a pioneer of June, 1849; President of the Pioneers, 1872-73; of Donahue, Booth & Co., foundrymen, 1863-65; President Omnibus Street R. R. Co., 1865-67; President S. F. & North Pacific Coast R. R. Co., 1870-71; President S. F. Gas Co., 1871-73; President of Gas Co., Omnibus Street R. R. Co., and State Investment Insurance Co., 1875; of two last named companies down to 1880; same and also of Sonoma Valley R. R. Co., 1881-83; presented St. Patrick's Catholic Church with a chime of bells, March 12, 1870; was born in Glasgow, Scotland, of Irish parents, Jan. 11, 1822; died at S. F., Nov. 26, 1885; left an estate appraised at $3,798,312.

Donahue, Mrs. Annie; widow of Peter Donahue, and sister of the late ex-Gov. John G. Downey, died Dec. 12, 1896; a native of Ireland, aged 60; funeral from St. Mary's Cathedral. Mrs. D. left a vast estate. See Supplement.

Donohoe, Denis; was H. B. M. Consul for the Pacific Coast, residing at S. F., from Jan. 6, 1887 to March, 1895, when he resigned, and retired to San Rafael, where he died Dec. 11, 1896, aged 71.

Donohoe, Jr., Denis; son of the preceding; was born in Buffalo, N. Y., Sept. 19, 1861; was educated at Loyola College, Baltimore, Md., Bishop's College, Lennoxville, Canada, University of Bonn, Germany, and Columbia College Law School, N. Y., graduating from the last named in the class of 1882; admitted to the bar in Poughkeepsie, N. Y., May 18, 1883; located in S. F. in the winter of 1888-89, and has since practiced, in partnership with T. E. K. Cormac, (C. & D.).

Donohoe, Joseph A.; influential citizen; a member of the pioneer banking house of Eugene Kelly & Co.; Donohoe, Ralston & Co., after June 1, 1861; Donohoe, Kelly & Co., after July 1, 1864; was a member of the Board of Health in 1866; and a School Director in 1868, which latter office he resigned, Jan. 14, 1868.

Donohoe, Kelly & Co.; Banking house of, was established July 1, 1864.

Donohoe, Kelly & Co.'s old Bank building, S. E. corner of Montgomery and Sacramento streets, was completed in the summer of 1864; of brick and stone: cost of lot and building, $125,000.

Donohoe, Ralston & Co.; Banking house of, was established June 1, 1861, and continued until July 1, 1864, when it was dissolved, Mr. Ralston having organized the Bank of California. See Mr. D.'s letter to Bulletin on March 24, 1887.

Donohoe Building; fine brick structure of seven stories, corner Market and Taylor streets, Joseph A. Donohoe, owner, was completed in 1891.

Donohoe-Kelly Banking Company was incorporated March 1, 1891; Joseph A. Donohoe, president; Joseph A. Donohoe, Jr., secretary.

Doolan, William; was Public Administrator, 1878-79.

Dom Pedro, Emperor of Brazil; arrived overland, April 25, 1876.

Donovan, M. J.; was School Director, 1871-75; and State Senator, 1875-76; 1877-78.

Dore, Maurice; old and prominent citizen; a leading auctioneer, and operator in real estate; died Oct. 3, 1895. His son, Charles, died at Auburn, of consumption, Feb. 27, 1888.

Dorn, Marcellus A.; prominent lawyer; was born in Los Angeles, Cal., Aug. 18, 1857; graduated from the University of California in 1879, and from Hastings Law College in 1882; was admitted to the bar of the Supreme Court, May 31, 1882; and located in S. F. on that day; since has practiced in partnership with his younger brother, D. S. Dorn (D. & D.). This firm had the legal business of the Sheriff of S. F. (C. S. Laumeister), for four years, 1889-92. A brother of these gentlemen, Hon. N. A. Dorn, is Superior Judge of Monterey County, elected in 1892.

Dorr L. L.; prominent physician and surgeon; was City and County Coroner for two terms, 1878-81; has been in active medical practice since 1873.

Dorr, Ralph S.; pioneer of Dec. 1, 1849; well-known broker; was President Board of Aldermen, in 1851; died Jan. 30, 1869, aged 62; a native of Mass.

Douthitt, D. Wm.; a pioneer of 1849; was born in Tenn., Sept. 28, 1828; admitted to the bar at Portland, Oregon, in 1857; was City Attorney of Portland; removed to Idaho, in 1864; to S. F., in 1868; was founder and first President of the " United Bar."

"Dow, Jr." (Elbridge Gerry Paige); for his wretched end, see press of Dec. 5, 1859.

Dow, William A.; was born in Sutter Co., Cal., Jan. 3, 1866; educated at the High School of Oakland, and at the State University; was admitted to the bar of the Supreme Court, at Sacramento, Nov. 11, 1890, and has since practiced in S. F. Resides in Oakland, where he has been a member of the City Council.

Dowling, Bartholomew; editor of the Catholic weekly, "The Monitor," died Nov. 20, 1863.

Doyle, John T.; distinguished lawyer; graduated from Georgetown College, D. C., in 1837, taking first honors; began law practice in N. Y. City, in 1842; was Superintendent of the Nicaragua Canal Co., in 1850; came to S. F., in 1851; returned to N. Y. City in 1856; to S. F. again in 1859, and has ever since been in the front rank at the bar; was a member of the Railroad Commission, or Commissioners of Transportation, 1876; of the Committee of One Hundred, in 1871. Mr. D. is a native of N. Y. City. A notice of his career forms Chapter XI of "Bench and Bar in California."

An article by Mr. D., on the Pious Fund of California, is in the Overland Monthly for Sept., 1890. A long interview with him, on the subject of Nicaragua and the Great Canal, is in the Bulletin of July 2, 1891. For his suggestions on " Printing the Public Records;" see the same paper, June 19, 1873.

Mrs. Elizabeth Pons, mother of Mrs. John T. Doyle, died at Mr. D.'s residence, at Menlo Park, Sept. 3, 1888, aged 81.

Draymen and Teamsters Union of S. F., was organized Aug. 26, 1876.

Druids, United Ancient Order of ; San Francisco Grove was organized, March 27, 1864.

The Druids' Library Association was organized, July 6, 1867.

The Druids' Hall Society was incorporated, Nov. 7, 1868.

Corner stone of the Hall, on Sutter street near Stockton, was laid, Oct. 25, 1869.

Dry Dock, San Francisco; was established at Rincon Point, in 1851; Neefus & Tichenor, proprietors.

Dry Goods Men's Association of S. F., was organized, Sept. 2, 1884.

Duane, Charles P.; was Chief Engineer of the Volunteer Fire Dep't, 1853-54. It was on account of Gov. Bigler's pardon of him for an assault on one Ball, that the grand jury appeared before County Judge Campbell, on Sept. 10, 1851, and demanded to be discharged. The Judge refused their request. The fatal shooting of Col. Wm. G. Ross, with whom Duane disputed about the ownership of a piece of land, occurred on May 23, 1866; D. was tried in the 12th District Court, and acquitted on Oct. 31, 1866. In the Assembly, in 1855, D. presented a portrait of Henry Clay to that body; that was the only California Assembly which ever had a Whig speaker (W. W. Stow). On Feb. 13, 1856, Silas Selleck, a Know Nothing Assemblyman from Placer, afterwards a well-known resident of S. F., moved to have this portrait of Clay removed, as being a caricature; the motion was lost. Duane died at S. F., May 13, 1887; he was a native of Tipperary, Ireland, aged 58. A graphic account by Duane with some amusing features, of the duel between David C. Broderick and J. Caleb Smith, at Oakland, in 1852, is in Ben. Truman's " Field of Honor." Broderick's pistol was borrowed from Duane, and had been presented to the latter by John A. McGlynn, in 1850.

Duels: Will Hicks Graham and Geo. Frank Lemon fought with pistols near the barracks at Benicia, Sept. 14, 1851; seven shots were exchanged; L. was badly hurt at the last fire.

Capt. J. L. Folsom and A. C. Russell, the latter a journalist of S. F., exchanged two shots, in 1851, without harm, and a settlement followed. Russell and Gov. John McDougal exchanged shots the same year, also without damage.

Gov. McDougal and E. C. Kemble, editor of the Alta, were about to face each other in 1851, but were arrested on the field.

F. R. Wright and H. D. Evans exchanged shots without harm, when the seconds arranged a peace, in 1851.

E. B. Lundy, a Canadian, and Geo. M. Dibble, formerly a midshipman in the U. S. N., met near the city, in 1851, with pistols. Dibble was killed.

Edward Gilbert (editor of the Alta, and ex-member of Congress) and James W. Denver (Senator from Trinity Co.), fought near Sacramento City, and Gilbert was shot and killed, Aug. 2, 1852.

Will Hicks Graham and William Walker met with pistols, in 1852, and Walker was dangerously wounded. He survived, to become the most famous filibuster of the century.

John Nugent and Wm. H. Jones met with pistols, in 1852, and Jones was slightly wounded.

William Leggett and John Morrison met near the city with pistols, in 1852. Leggett was killed at the third fire.

A. C. Peachy, the eminent lawyer, wounded James Blain in a duel with pistols, in 1852.

John Kelley and W. S. Spear fired at each other, three times, without effect, in 1852.

David C. Broderick and J. Caleb Smith fought in 1852, at a spot which is now the foot of Broadway, Oakland. They used navy revolvers, at ten paces. S. escaped injury, but one of his shots struck the watch in B.'s pocket, and the fragments of the watch slightly cut B.'s stomach; this was S.'s second shot, and B. received it while he was engaged in freeing the cylinder of his pistol from the exploded cap which had caught in it; both parties then emptied all their barrels, after which the seconds established peace. So many people had gone to the duelling ground from S. F., in small boats, all through the previous night, that they could not all get back the same way without great delay, and many secured horses and got home by way of San José. Chas. P. Duane's account of this duel, and of the laughable part he played in connection with it, is to be found in Ben Truman's "Field of Honor."

John Nugent, lawyer and editor, and Alderman John Cotter fought with pistols at ten paces, in 1852, in Contra Costa County; N. was severely wounded in the left thigh, at the second fire.

John Nugent and Assistant Alderman Thos. Hayes fought with rifles at twenty paces, in 1853, and again N. was wounded at the second shot.

Alfred Crane and Edward Tobey fought with navy revolvers at ten paces near S. F., in 1853. Crane, who was the challenged party, was shot through the body, and died the next day.

Edward Rowe and Col. May met in 1853, and Rowe was wounded in the neck.

Wm. H. Scott and Peter Smith (a son of Judge Pinckney Smith of Miss.) fought with pistols at eighteen paces, in 1853. Smith was killed at the second fire.

C. J. Wright and Oliver T. Baird met near S. F. with pistols, in 1853. B. was wounded in the neck at the second fire.

Dr. James P. Dixon, of the S. F. Marine Hospital, and Philip F. Thomas, District Attorney of Placer Co., met with duelling pistols, at thirteen paces, three miles from Sacramento, in March, 1854. Dr. Dixon received a wound, from which he soon died.

David E. Hacker and J. S. Londen fought in 1854, and Londen was killed.

M. C. Brazer and J. W. Park fought in 1854, without result.

B. F. Washington and C. A. Washburn fought with rifles at forty paces, in 1854; Washburn was severely wounded at the second fire. He was afterwards, under the first administration of President Lincoln, Minister to Paraguay. Washington, in 1854, was editor of the Times and Transcript; he became Collector of the Port, under President Buchanan, and afterwards edited the Examiner.

Geo. T. Hunt, English, and Numa Hubert, French, both prominent lawyers, fought with pistols at the old Pioneer race course, at 5:30 A. M. May 21, 1854. Hunt, the challenged party, fell at the third fire. He called Hubert to him, and said "I forgive you." He died in 24 hours. An account of this duel and its occasion, by O. T. S., is in the Post of March 4, 1882. And see "Hubert, Numa."

Achilles Kewen, brother of E. J. C. Kewen, and Col. Woodlief, ex-County Judge of San Joaquin, had a political dispute in the Blue Wing saloon, on Montgomery street near Clay, in Nov., 1854. K. acknowledged that he had been too hasty, but W. would not accept this, and insisted on a fight. They met ten miles back of Oakland, Nov. 8th, and at the first fire, which was with Mississippi yagers, at forty paces, W. was shot in the head and killed instantly.

Austin E. Smith, a brother of Judge Smith, who had fought with Broderick, and H. B. Truett met near the city, in Oct., 1855, with Colt's revolvers, ten paces. S. was hit in the leg.

Jas. P. Withered and Capt. Frank Shaffer met with double-barrelled shot guns, loaded with buck shot, near S. F., in 1857. The formidable arms did no damage.

A. H. Rapp, editor of the French paper, Le Phare, and M. Thiele, editor of the French paper, Spectateur, fought with short swords, Jan. 27, 1858; T. was wounded in the leg.

Balie Peyton and Gregory Yale, distinguished lawyers, while on the field near Oakland, and about to exchange shots, received a letter from Francis J. Lippitt, a brother attorney, who was connected with the trouble, which brought about an immediate settlement, June 18, 1858.

Wm. I. Ferguson, lawyer and orator of first rank, State Senator from Sacramento, and Geo. Pen. Johnston, Clerk of the U. S. Circuit Court, and associate editor of the National, had a convivial altercation in the Bank Exchange saloon, Aug. 19, 1858; a duel with pistols followed on Angel Island, Aug. 21st; F.'s thigh bone

was broken at the fourth fire; he died at S. F., Sept. 14, 1858. For
an account of the affair and Ferguson's interesting life, see "Representative Men."

Wm. I. Ferguson's last moments; his noble nature; a pathetic
recital; see Sacramento "Union," Sept. 17, 1858, page 2.

David C. Broderick, U. S. Senator, and David S. Terry, Justice
of the Supreme Court, fought with pistols, near Lake Merced,
S. F., Sept. 13, 1859; B. fell at the first fire, and died Sept. 16th.
For a graphic account by an eye witness, see "Bench and Bar."

Chas. W. Piercy, of San Bernardino, and Daniel Showalter
of Mariposa, both members of the Assembly, fought in Marin Co.
with rifles, and Piercy was killed, May 25, 1861.

Frank Turk and O. C. Hall, lawyers, exchanged shots, then
"made up," June 1, 1862.

For correspondence looking to a duel, between Hon. Wm. W.
Porter and Hon. H. G. Worthington—Wm. Governeur Morris and
James E. Nuttman, representing W., and Jas. F. Quin and David
S. Terry, representing P.—See local papers, June 23, 24, 1861.

A German and a Pole fought in the dark, with revolvers, at 12
paces, at 7 o'clock, P. M., Nov. 28, 1866; neither was hurt.

James R. Smedberg and F. W. Gardener fought at Sausalito
with duelling pistols in Aug., 1869; S. was wounded in the hand at
the second fire. His second was Col. Stuart M. Taylor; while
Howard Crittenden attended Gardener. In this, one of the latest, if
not the very latest duel in California, both parties displayed great
nerve.

Paul Zacchi and one Ives met near the Ocean House, Jan. 19,
1875; Z. instead of aiming at his adversary, tried to kill himself.
Both parties survived.

Major Ben C. Truman, in his "Field of Honor," issued in
1884, declares that there have been more fatal duels in California
than in all of the Northern States; and that between the years of
1850 and 1860, more fatal encounters took place in this State than
elsewhere in the Union in any ten years' period.

In the foregoing record, duels occurring in the interior are
not noticed except where one or both participants belonged to
San Francisco.

Baker's eloquent protest against the "Code of Honor," was
uttered in his oration at the burial of Broderick, Sept. 18, 1859.
(This noble oration is in "Representative Men of the Pacific.")

Dufferin, Earl, Gov.-Gen'l of Canada, arrived Aug. 8, 1876.

Duhring, Frederick T.; was born in Sonoma, Cal., Sept. 2, 1862; was educated in the public schools, the Napa Collegiate Institute, and
the State University; and was admitted to the bar at S. F., Aug.
5, 1890.

Dun, R. G. & Co.'s, Mercantile Agency; S. F. branch was established in
1869, the office being at 224 Sansome street, under the management of James A. Dun. The firm composing the Agency was

made up of R. Graham Dun, Charles Barlow, M. B. Smith and Erastus Wiman, all residing in N. Y. Mr. Jay Lugsdin has been manager of the S. F. office ever since 1870.

For the Bradstreet Co. Mercantile Agency, see Supplement.

Duncan, Joseph C.; his bank, the "Pioneer Land and Loan Bank of Savings and Deposits" failed, causing widespread distress, Oct. 7, 1877; Duncan went into hiding, and was suprised and captured at night by Capt. Lees, in the building 509 Kearny street, Feb. 24, 1878; he was indicted on ten charges of forgery, embezzlement, and grand larceny; was released on bail in $61,500, Aug. 14, 1880; the first of his abortive trials began in the Municipal Criminal Court, Dec. 16, 1878; the evidence being insufficient to convict, the last of the charges was dismissed on motion of the District Attorney, Jan. 6, 1882.

Dundon, P. F.; proprietor of the S. F. Iron Works (before 1894, the S. F. Boiler Works), of Dundon's patent compound marine boilers, was a member of the Board of Supervisors, 1893-94. He is a boiler maker by trade, and was foreman for Moynihan & Aitken from 1877 to 1883, when he went into the business for himself.

Dunlevy Andrew J.; veteran police officer; was dangerously stabbed by Frank Schwartz, Sept. 17, 1871. This officer has been on the force since 1868, when he was aged 42; his previous occupation was that of a ship carpenter; he is a native of Ireland.

Dunphy, William; a pioneer of Dec. 27, 1849; a great cattle raiser and dealer for thirty years.

See the peculiar case of Nichols vs. Dunphy, 53rd vol. California Reports, page 654. A daughter of D. married Samuel W. Piercy, the actor; another married Noah F. Flood, lawyer.

Dunn, John P.; was Auditor of the City and County, appointed to fill a vacancy in Nov., 1879, and elected for the years 1880-81, on the Workingmen's ticket; was State Controller for two terms, Jan., 1883 to Jan. 5, 1891; Secretary of the Citizens' Defense Association at S. F., in 1892-93; Register of the U. S. Land office at S. F., in 1895-97.

Dunn, Thos. F.; who has been Assistant District Attorney under Hon. Wm. S. Barnes since 1893; was born in Buffalo, N. Y., May 22, 1871; came to S. F. in 1876; educated at St. Ignatius College, S. F.; admitted to the bar of the State Supreme Court, Oct. 10, 1892.

Dunn, Horace D.; an old and respected citizen; now and since 1890, an expert accountant, was a commission merchant in early days; a reporter for the Bulletin in 1863-64; State Commissioner of Immigration, 1866-70; acting Consul for Japan, 1873-74; a member of the Board of Education, and Chairman of the judiciary committee in 1882 (term was then one year). He is author of an elaborate essay on the agricultural resources of this State, written for the U. S. Commissioners of Agriculture, and copied in appendix 3 to the legislative journals, 1867-68, and commended in the preface to that vol.; also author of an article on the introduction of lobsters in S. F. Bay—Bulletin, March 29, 1882; an article on rice culture, in same paper, Sept. 27, 1890; and many other writings of general interest. Mr. D. registered June 1, 1866, as a reporter, born in N. Y., aged 36.

Dunne, Joseph J.; well-known lawyer; was a Justice of the Peace in the years, 1883-84; Assistant District Attorney, 1887-88; and Prosecuting Attorney Police Court No. 1, 1889-90.

Dunne, Peter F.; an advocate noted for his polished and logical addresses to Court and jury, grew up in S. F., graduated from the Hastings Law College, and was admitted to the bar of the Supreme Court in 1882; he practiced alone until 1889, when the present law firm of Dunne & McPike was formed (Peter F. Dunne, Henry C. McPike and Joseph J. Dunne, the last named withdrawing in 1894).

Dupont Street Widening; Dupont street was widened from Market to Bush streets to a uniform width of seventy-four feet, under Act of legislature of March 23rd, 1876; litigation began in 1879, in the name of Wm. M. Lent et al. vs. Tillson, Tax Collector, to have the assessment of real estate under the Act declared void; the U. S. Supreme Court decided in favor of the validity of the Act and affirmed the proceedings and assessment under it, on May 11, 1892; but thereafter other suits were instituted and are not yet determined. But the street was actually widened from Market to Bush streets as called for by the Act, the work being completed in 1886. . On July, 31, 1886, the name of that portion of the street was changed to Grant Avenue by the Board of Supervisors. (Order No. 1872.)

"Dupont Street Frauds;" see local papers, June 13th and Sept. 28, 1882, and intermediate dates.

Durant, Henry; President of the University of California, and who selected the site at Berkeley, died Aug. 16, 1870.

Durkee, John L.; was Fire Marshal of the Board of Underwriters from May 26, 1864 until Oct. 15, 1886, when he was retired on a life pension of $100 per month. He wrote an article, in Bulletin, July 17, 1888, giving a history of the bells of his old Engine Co., Monumental, No. 6. He died Jan. 29, 1897; a native of Baltimore, Md., aged 69; his funeral was from St. Bridget's Catholic Church.

Durrant, Wm. H. T.; a student at Cooper Medical College, aged 24, residing with his parents on Fair Oaks street, was tried for the murder of Blanche Lamont, a school girl, aged 21, in 1895, the trial beginning on July 22nd, and ending on Nov. 1st, 1895, when he was convicted of murder in the first degree, in Judge D. J. Murphy's Department t of the Superior Court; sentence of death was passed on Dec. 7th. Blanche Lamont disappeared on April 3, 1895; her body was found in the belfry of Emmanuel Baptist Church, April 14, 1895. On April 12, 1895, Miss Minnie Williams was killed in the same church, and Durrant was also indicted for her murder. The appeal of the accused, from the judgment of condemnation for the murder of Blanche Lamont, was submitted to the Supreme

Court on Oct. 21, 1896. The points and authorities were filed Dec. 7, 1896. On March 3, 1897, the Supreme Court, in an opinion written by Justice Henshaw, and signed by all the Justices except Chief Justice Beatty, who gave no expression, affirmed the judgment of guilty. See Supplement.

Durst, John H.; was City and County Attorney, Election Commissioner, and City Hall Commissioner, in 1891-92; was born in Sacramento. He located and began law practice in S. F., in 1884. The firm of Nygh, Fairweather & Durst, was formed in 1885, Mr. D. withdrawing after two years.

Dutch, William; distinguished dentist; died by his own hand by hanging, in his office, Oct. 24, 1887.

Dutton, Henry; long established hay dealer; influential member of the Produce Exchange, died Dec 4, 1887; was President of the Farmers and Mechanics Bank of Savings, from 1868 until the bank went into liquidation in 1880.

Dutton, Wm. J.; son of the preceding; after a long period of service as Secretary of the Firemen's Fund Insurance Co., became vice President of the company in 1890; and in 1895, President of the Home Mutual Insurance Co. He was born in Maine, Jan. 23, 1847, and came to S. F. in 1853.

Dutton, Warren; prominent citizen; a pioneer of Aug. 1, 1849. See "Dairymen's Union."

Dwinelle, John W.; distinguished lawyer; a pioneer of Oct., 1849; was mysteriously drowned at Port Costa, Jan. 28, 1881. On Feb. 1, 1850, his name led the petition of a number of S. F. lawyers, praying the legislature to retain the Civil Law in its substantial elements, as proposed by Gov. Burnett in his first message, in preference to adopting the English Common Law. Among many able public addresses, perhaps the most interesting was that which he delivered at the laying of the corner stone of the New City Hall, Dec. 28, 1871. For his "Judicial Trial of Jesus," see Bulletin, March 6, 1877. He made his home in Oakland, and represented Alameda County in the Assembly, 1867-68. He was a native of N. Y., and attained the age of 62.

Dwinelle, Samuel H.; brother of the preceding, was Judge of the Fifteenth District Court, for S. F. and Contra Costa, from the organization of the Court in 1864, until it ceased to exist, at the close of 1879. He died suddenly, of apoplexy, Jan. 12, 1886, aged 61 years and 11 months; a native of N. Y.

E

Eagle Block, N. W. corner Pine and Davis streets, was built for A. B. McCreary, at a cost of $160,000; the work was begun in Jan., 1882, and completed in May, same year.

Earthquakes: there were 21 shocks at the Presidio between June 21st and July 17, 1808.

The shock of Jan. 16, 1856 was the severest up to that time, since the American occupation; it occurred in the latter part of the night, and was announced by a loud report, like a steam boiler explosion.

Three severe shocks occurred on Feb. 26, 1864.

There were several severe shocks on May 20, 1864.

A severe shock occurred at 3 o'clock A. M., May 24, 1865, which extended some distance down the coast.

A shock which shattered the walls of many buildings and did great damage, occurrred on Sunday, Oct. 8, 1865; it was felt over a wide area, brick buildings being injured in Santa Cruz, San José and other towns; there were two shocks the next day, which did no damage.

There were two severe shocks at 12:20 P. M., March 26, 1866.

A severe chock on May 30, 1866.

Quite a severe shock was felt at 11:30 A. M., March 24, 1868.

The most violent earthquake experienced in the City and State since the American settlement of the country, occurred at 7:54 A. M., Oct. 21, 1868. The first and heavier shock was felt for about forty-five seconds, and was followed by others of shorter duration during the day. Several persons were killed by falling walls, and others were seriously injured. Three or four buildings were thrown down, and a large number were badly damaged. The loss in property was estimated at half a million dollars.

Easterby, Capt. A. Y.; who is said to have landed at S. F. on Christmas Day, 1848, but who, according to the Pioneer records, arrived on Jan. 10, 1849; died at Napa, in June, 1893. A valuable article on the compass in relation to iron ships, giving his experiments in the Levant, is in the Bulletin of Aug. 2, 1890.

Eastern Star, Order of; the Grand Chapter was organized May 9, 1873; the first Subordinate Chapter, was instituted on May 9, 1869.

Eastland, Joseph G.; influential and wealthy citizen; secretary of the S. F. Gas Co., 1855 to 1878; New City Hall Commissioner, 1870-74; President of the Pioneers, two terms, 1880-82; Trustee of the Beideman Life Trust, which he resigned March 5, 1888; President S. F. High License Association, 1892; arrived in California, Dec. 1, 1849; died in 1895, a native of Tenn., aged 63.

Eastland, Major Thos. B.; Mexican war veteran, and a pioneer of Nov., 1849; died Nov. 11, 1864, aged 58.

Easton, Oliver W.; father of Wendell and George Easton, died on Nov. 6, 1881; a native of Mass., aged 66.

Easton, Wendell; founder of the real estate firm of Easton, Eldridge & Co.; was bookkeeper for Madison & Burke, 1867-72; bookkeeper of the Crown Point Mining Co., 1874; mining secretary, 1875-77; of Easton & De Forest, real estate, 1878; continued that business alone, under the style of Easton & Co., 1879-80. Established the house of Easton & Eldridge, with J. O. Eldridge, in 1881—real estate agents and auctioneers; on the death of Mr. Eldridge, Feb. 26, 1885, Mr. Easton continued the business without change of style until 1887, when the house of Easton, Eldridge & Co., was incorporated, with Mr. E. as President, Geo. W. Frink, Vice President, Frank B. Wilde, Secretary, and the Anglo-Californian Bank, treasurer. In 1892, Mr. Geo. Easton succeeded Mr. Wilde as secretary, at the same time continuing as head of the insurance firm of Geo. Easton & Co. In 1894, Geo. Easton became Vice President reta'ning for a year the secretaryship. In 1895, he was succeeded as secretary by Geo. D. Easton; and he also retired from his other house (insurance). In 1894-95, Wendell Easton, in addition to the presidency of this corporation (E. E. & Co.) was President of the Pacific Coast Savings Society, and of the Metropolitan Railway Co.

Mr. Wendell Easton was the Republican candidate for Mayor in 1894. He registered as a voter, June 12, 1896, as born in Mass., aged 48.

Easton, Eldridge & Co., see "Easton, Wendell."

Ebbets, A. M.; a pioneer of Aug. 5, 1849; County Recorder in 1861; Supervisor in 1874-75; proprietor of the Merchants' Coal Yard since 1867; Mr. Ebbets was born in N. Y. City, on Jan. 18, 1830; during all the exciting history of the City since its earliest days, his residence has serenely stood on the commanding site, at the N. W. corner of Jones and Washington Streets, and there it stands still, a most remarkable illustration of conservatism in residence.

"Echo du Pacifique," daily French newspaper, was established in June, 1852.

Eclipse of the Sun, partial, occurred May 5, 1864.

Eclipse of the Sun, partial, occurred Aug. 7, 1869; lasted two hours.

"Eco del Pacifico," daily Spanish newspaper, was established in June, 1852.

Edgerton, Henry; lawyer and distinguished orator; was excelled as a public speaker only by E. D. Baker and Thos. Fitch; born in Vt., in 1830; came to Cal. in 1853; was State Senator from Napa, Solano and Yolo, 1860-61; same from Sacramento, 1873-74; 1875-76; was author of the Broderick Expunging Resolutions, Jan. 19, 1861; one of the three counsel for the State in the impeachment of Judge Jas. H. Hardy, May, 1862; resided in S. F. at different times, for short periods; died at S. F. suddenly, while on a visit, in a lawyer's office, Nov. 4, 1887.

Edwards, Henry; versatile actor, and entomologist; made his home in S. F. from 1868 to 1879; in 1868-69, was lessee and manager of the Metropolitan Theater; President of the Bohemian Club, and a director of the Art Association, 1873-74; made the presentation speech on behalf of Miss Lotta Crabtree, when the Lotta Fountain was formally delivered to the City, Sept. 9, 1875; was author of a work on " Butterflies of the Pacific Coast;" his private collection of insects numbered over 60,000 specimens, estimated to be worth $20,000. He was born in England in 1830; left California in 1879; died many years ago. A notice of his career is in the Post of Jan. 3, 1874.

Edwin, Sophie; a favorite emotional actress, wife of Wm. Stevenson, deputy County Clerk, who had been treasurer of Maguire's Opera House, where the actress became popular, died March 7, 1876.

Eells, Alex. G.; was born in Dayton, O., March 18, 1862, graduated from the University of California in 1886, and was admitted to the bar at S. F., in 1888.

Eells, James D. D.; distinguished Presbyterian divine, who had the pastorate of the First Presbyterian church in S. F., 1867-69, died in Cincinnati, Ohio, March 9, 1886, in his 64th year, being then a professor in Lane Theological Seminary.

An editorial notice of him is in the Bulletin of March 10, 1886. Dr. Eells was father of the well-known lawyer, Chas. P. Eells and Mrs. Horatio Livermore.

Eells, Chas. P.; son of the preceding; was born in N. Y., May 18, 1854; educated at the City College, S. F., the Oakland College, Poughkeepsie Military Academy, N. Y., and Hamilton College, Clinton, N. Y.; was admitted to the bar at Sacramento, April 11, 1877, and began practice at S. F. in 1879.

Eggers, Geo. H.; wholesale grocer; a pioneer of Aug. 14, 1849; was a member of the great Vigilance Committee of 1856; one of the founders of the German Savings Bank; a leading spirit in St. Mark's Lutheran Church; President of the Eggers Vineyard Co.; died May 22, 1896; a native of Hanover, aged 76; Masonic burial.

Eickhoff, Henry; well-known lawyer; was born in N. Y.; graduated from Columbia Law School; located and began law practice in S. F., in 1875.

"Elaine," Rosenthal's great picture, was cut from its frame and stolen, April 2, 1875. It was recovered, and six men were arrested for the theft, April 4, 1875. One of the thieves was sentenced to eight years in the State prison, May 29, 1875.

El Dorado County Pioneers, Society of, was organized Nov. 12, 1870.

Eldridge, J. O.; prominent auctioneer, one of the founders of the real estate house of Easton, Eldridge & Co., died Feb. 26, 1885; a native of Mass., aged 56. Some twenty years prior to his death, Mr. E. in the line of auctioneer, had the habit of slapping his leg with his hand as he announced a piece of property "sold." A disease of the bone was thus contracted, which necessitated the amputation of the leg.

Elks, California; 20 stags safely reached King Victor Emanuel, the gift of Californians, May 1, 1864; the whole cost $600.

Elks, Benevolent and Protective Order of, was organized April 11, 1876.

Ellinwood, Chas.; eminent physician and surgeon; was surgeon of the City and County Hospital since 1890, and Professor of Physiology in Cooper Medical College, since 1889; holding such professorship also in 1886-87; President U. S. Board of Pension Surgeons, 1884-85; surgeon and physician for the German Hospital, 1881-83; surgeon of the U. S. Marine Hospital, 1872-80; Professor of Physiology, Medical Dep't, University of the Pacific, 1872-73; began medical practice in S. F., in 1868. He registered on July 4, 1896, as born in Vt., aged 60.

Ellis, John S.; was Sheriff in 1862-63; resigned the office, May 2, 1864. He belonged to a distinguished N. Y. family, and returned to that State in 1864, and died there in 1896. His sister is the wife of Gen. John Hewston, Jr. His mother, Mrs. Elizabeth Van Horn Ellis, died at Gen. Hewston's country seat in Alameda County, in 1896, at the age of 92.

Ellis Land Case, affecting property worth over $4,000,000; trial opened in the Fourth District Court, Jan. 23, 1877; it ended with judgment for the defendants, Jan. 26, 1877.

"El Primero;" the first steam steel yacht built on the Pacific Coast, appeared on the bay, in July, 1893, built by the Union Iron Works for E. W. Hopkins. Dimensions: length over all, 137 feet; beam, 18 feet; depth, 8 feet 6 inches; mean draft, 4 feet 8 inches; registered tonnage, gross, 102.99 tons; net, 73.48; displacement, 70 tons. Picture in Californian Magazine, Oct., 1893.

Ellsworth, Oliver; has been at the S. F. bar since June 24, 1891, when he entered the profession; he is a graduate of the University of California, and of Hastings Law College; was born at Mission San José, Alameda Co., April 7, 1867.

Emeric, Joseph; pioneer of Dec. 29, 1849; on July 16, 1870, during the Franco-Prussian war, Mr. E. offered $500, to the French soldier who should be first to capture a Prussian flag; died June 22, 1889; native of France, aged 73; left a large estate.

Emeric, Henry F.; only son of the preceding; represented Contra Costa in the Assembly in 1893; registered July 17, 1871, as born in N. Y., aged 23.

Emmet, Christopher Temple; pioneer of 1849; distinguished lawyer; a grand nephew of Robert Emmet, the Irish patriot; was born in N. Y. City, in 1823; graduated as a physician and surgeon from the University of Va.; was admitted to the bar in N. Y.; practiced in S. F., from 1849 until 1867, when he left the profession with a fortune of a million dollars, and went into the California and Oregon Railway project of Ben. Holladay, in which he lost all; resumed practice in 1873; died in N. Y., and was buried on his place, comprising 60 acres, near San Rafael, Feb 27, 1884; a most interesting character; see sketch by O. T. S. in Bulletin, Feb. 28, 1884.

Emmet, Robert; the centennial of his birth was celebrated by overflowing houses in Metropolitan Temple and Pacific Hall, March 4, 1878.

Engine Companies No. 1 and No. 5, of the old volunteer Fire Department, was disbanded by order of the Board of Supervisors, upon complaint of Chief Engineer F. E. R. Whitney, for disobedience of his order at a fire, May 11, 1858; the companies were reinstated under a decision of Judge Norton, of the 12th District Court, May 29, 1858.

Enos, John S.; lawyer and eloquent speaker; State Senator, 1880-81; nominee of the Workingmen for Congress in 1882; withdrew in the middle of the campaign in favor of Gen. Rosecrans, Democrat, who was elected; was Commissioner of the State Bureau of Labor Statistics, 1883-86.

Ensign, George H.; who figured so prominently in the early history of the City's water supply, died at Stockton, Oct. 2, 1871.

Eoff, James L.; noted horse jockey; died Aug. 2, 1885, a native of N. J., aged 67. In a dispute about a horse race, E. shot and killed Wm. D. Chapman, in the Pony Saloon, Kearny street, Jan. 17, 1863; he was tried in the 12th District Court, and acquitted, May 1, 1863.

Epizootic, or Epizööty, The; made its first appearance in S. F. on April 16, 1873; on April 25th, it prevailed to such an extent as to seriously interfere with business and almost suspend car travel. Wells, Fargo & Co. used oxen in their freight wagons. The disease reappeared, in a milder form, in Nov., 1875.

Epworth League Alliance wes organized in May, 1893.

Escambia, British iron steamship, foundered on the bar, after passing out of the harbor, June 19, 1882. The Escambia Wrecking Co., was organized and incorporated July 15, 1882.

Estee, M. M.; distinguished lawyer; represented Sacramento to the Assembly, 1863; District Attorney of that County, 1864-65; represented S. F. in the Assembly, and was Speaker thereof, Dec. 1, 1873 to March 30, 1874; was the Republican caucus nominee for the U. S. Senate, when Farley, Democrat, was chosen, Dec. 19, 1877; candidate for Governor in 1882, when Gen. Stoneman was elected, and same in 1894, against Gov. Budd; President of the Republican National Convention in 1888; Member of the Pan American Congress in 1889-90; came to California in 1853; was admitted to the bar at Sacramento in 1860; removed to S. F. in 1866; born in Penn., Nov. 23, 1833; sketch in Bancroft's "Contemporary Biography."

Eugene Kelly & Co.; see Donohoe, Jos. A.

Eureka Typographical Union (No. 21 of the National Union), was organized Nov. 20, 1854; was admitted into the National Union, May 7, 1855.

Evans, Oliver P.; prominent lawyer; Judge of the Superior Court, Jan., 1880 to Aug. 1, 1883, when he resigned, to resume law practice; registered July 10, 1896, as born in Va., aged 54; located and began practice in S. F. in 1868; was in partnership with the eminent jurist, John Currey, from the time the latter left the Supreme bench to his, Judge C.'s, retirement from practice on the first of Jan., 1878, a period of eight years.

Examiner Newspaper; was established as an evening daily by Capt. Wm. S. Moss, of Stockton, on June 12, 1865. Philip A. Roach, and Chas. L. Weller purchased interests the following year; W. withdrew and Geo. Pen. Johnston and James Porter bought interests, in 1869.

The paper was sold in Oct., 1880, to W. T. Baggett & Co., who converted it into a morning daily; it was shortly transferred to the Examiner Publishing Co., composed of Hon. Geo. Hearst. W. R. Hearst became the owner on March 4, 1887.

Exempt Fire Company was organized Dec. 8, 1862, under the Act of the legislature, approved March 26, 1857, for social intercourse and mutual benefit; it was reorganized April 15, 1872, under Act of March 14, 1872.

Explosions: A large tank in the California Sugar Refinery burst Jan. 6, 1859, shattering the building, and killing an employe named Calcott.

An explosion on the steamboat Diana, off Vallejo Street wharf, Dec. 27, 1860, fatally injured Wm. Shaw, the engineer and Thos. Johnson, a hand.

Boiler of engine of the National Flouring Mills, at Market and Sansome streets, burst on Oct. 25, 1862, fatally injuring four men.

The steamer Washoe burst her boiler 40 miles below Sacramento Sept. 6, 1864; 100 persons were killed.

The steamboat Sophie McLane blew up at Suisun, Oct. 26, 1864, killing Capt. Geo. Folger, pilot, Chas. Yates, 2nd engineer, Wm. Lawler, deckhand, and Henry P. Hulbert.

The steamboat Yosemite exploded her boiler at Rio Vista, blowing off the entire forward portion of the boat, Oct. 13, 1865; a large number of persons were killed and wounded.

A terrible explosion of a case of nitro-glycerine occurred on April 16, 1866, in the yard adjoining Wells, Fargo & Co.'s Express office, then located in the stone building at the northwest corner of Montgomery and California streets. Several persons were killed, among them being Samuel Knight, Sup't of W., F. & Co., and G. W. Bell, assayer and member of the Board of Supervisors. Thirteen deaths resulted, the last, that of Miss Emily Treadwell, occurring at Santa Rosa, on July 1, 1866.

The steam drum of the steamer Julia burst at Broadway wharf, Sept. 29, 1866, killing four of the hands.

An explosion of gas at the (old) St. Nicholas Hotel severely wounded three men, Jan. 6, 1869.

An explosion and fire occurred at the Giant Powder Works
west of the cemeteries, Nov. 26, 1869, which totally destroyed the
Works, and killed ten Chinese workmen.

An explosion at the Giant Powder Works on July 9, 1870, killed the Sup't, John Harry.

An explosion at the Giant Powder Works on June 21, 1872, did
much damage.

An explosion of gasoline, at the warehouse of Whittier, Fuller
& Co., did considerable damage, April 4, 1872.

Explosion of gas from the street main on Mission street, seriously injured three men, June 27, 1872.

Explosion of gas on Harrison Street Wharf, April 7, 1875,
caused the loss of four lives and the destruction of Hathaway's
warehouse and other buildings.

Explosion at the Bay View Distillery occurred Sept. 26, 1874,
killing one workman.

Explosion of giant powder on the Potrero occurred Aug. 15,
1877.

Exposition, California International Midwinter, was formally opened in
Golden Gate Park ("Sunset City"), S. F., Jan. 27, 1894.

F

Fabbri Opera Troupe produced the opera of Joseph in Egypt, at Wade's
Opera House, on Feb. 6, 1876.

Fabbri, Prof. Mulder; long connected with the musical profession; died
Dec. 22, 1874, aged 52.

Fabens, F. A.; well-known lawyer, who had been in partnership with F. P.
Tracy (F. & T.) in 1858-59, died suddenly at Sausalito, while holding the office of Justice of the Peace at S. F., June 16, 1872, aged 58.

Fair, James G.; pioneer of Sept. 3, 1849; was U. S. Senator from Nevada,
March 4, 1881 to March 4, 1887; became President of the Nevada
Bank of S. F., Sept. 13, 1887, in place of James C. Flood, resigned;
fixed his residence at S. F. in 1887; sold the South Pacific Coast
R. R. to the S. P. Co., in March, 1887; bought the Lick House of
the Lick trustees for $1,250,000, Oct. 5, 1888; invested about
$1,000,000 in lots and erection of buildings on the water front, north
of Clay street, 1889-90; awarded to Warren and Malley contract for
$300,000, for grading many blocks of land at the North End, be-
tween Webster and Baker streets, June 23, 1893. Mr. Fair died at

the Lick House, which was one of his possessions, on Dec. 29, 1894; his estate, believed to be worth at least $25,000,000, had not been appraised when this volume was printed. The final account of the special administrators was filed Dec. 9, 1896, giving the value of the estate as $16,633,455. For Mr. Fair's views on Adolph Sutro, the Sutro Tunnel, and the Silver question, see Bulletin, March 12, 1893, page 4.

Mr. Fair bought of O. F. Giffen the two fifty-vara lots, N. W. Pine and Jones street, with the fine mansion and furniture, for $130,000, Feb. 2, 1879.

Fair, Mrs. Theresa; the estate left by her and accounted for by her executors, Jno. W. Mackay and R. V. Dey, in their final account, July 13, 1893, was $5,096, 646.

Fair, Mrs. Laura D.; appeared at the Metropolitan Theater at Sacramento, as Lady Teazle, in School for Scandal, March 5, 1863; had a fine reception at the Metropolitan Theater, S. F., March 13, 1863; shot the distinguished lawyer, A. P. Crittenden, on the Oakland ferry boat, Nov. 3, 1870; her trial on an indictment for murder, was begun in the 15th District Court, Hon. S. H. Dwinelle presiding, March 27, 1871; a verdict of murder in the first degree was rendered on the 26th day of the trial; on June 3, the defendant was sentenced to be hung on July 28, 1871; she appealed, was granted a new trial, and was tried a second time in the same Court, Hon. Thos. B. Reardon, of the 14th District, Nevada and Placer Counties, presiding in place of Judge Dwinelle; a verdict of not guilty was rendered, Sept. 30, 1872, and she was discharged.

Fair, Wm. D.; prominent lawyer; a pioneer of June 22, 1849; State Senator from San Joaquin Co. at the first session, 1849-50; removed to S. F., and died by his own hand, in his office, Dec. 27, 1861. Was the husband of Laura D. Fair. Col. Fair was a good lawyer, and a man of splendid presence, a native of Va.; graduate of West Point; and was for some years an army officer. He married Mrs. Fair, who was then Mrs. Grayson, at Shasta, Cal., in 1859.

Fairchild, John; scenic artist; died Feb. 9, 1862.

Falkner, Bell & Co.; commission merchants and insurance agents, were established in 1852.

Fallon, Thomas; a pioneer of March 8, 1844; died Oct. 25, 1885, a native of Ireland, aged 67; left an estate worth $200,000.

Farmers and Mechanics Bank of Savings was ordered into liquidation by the Bank Commissioners, Sept. 3, 1878.

Farnsworth, Dr. A. A.; died by his own hand, April 15, 1874.

Farquharson, David; eminent architect; President of the California Savings and Loan Society, and of the Visitation Water Co.; was architect for the College of Letters and the College of Agriculture, University buildings at Berkeley, in 1872-74; was defeated by I. S. Kalloch for Mayor, in 1879; began his prosperous professional career in S. F., in 1862; registered June 30, 1866, as born in Scotland, aged 39.

Farren, John W.; who was a Supervisor in 1878-79, and who died in March, 1896, was one of the carriage making firm of Clapp and Farren, which began business on Jan. 1, 1853; the style of the firm was changed to Farren & Eaton, May 1, 1856.

Farwell, J. D.; organized the Pacific Cordage Co., in 1877; arrived at S. F. in the spring of 1850, and engaged extensively in ship chandlery; he was a member of the Vigilance Committees of 1851 and 1856, and Vice President of the last; died at Haywards, Nov. 19, 1887; a native of Me., aged 72.

Farwell, Willard B.; pioneer of July 6, 1849; Assemblyman in 1855; edited the Alta in 1858-59; President of the Pioneers, in 1863-64; Naval Officer under President Lincoln, 1861-65; Supervisor, 1885-86. Mr. F. delivered the annual oration before the Society of California Pioneers, Sept. 9, 1859. He is a native of Mass.

Farallone Islands were discovered by Bartolome Ferrelo, a Portuguese navigator in the service of Spain, in 1543; they were first specially mentioned by Sir Francis Drake, in 1579; these islands are composed of three groups; the middle is a single rock; the northerly is made up of five rocks; the southerly, the largest, is two miles around, has the lighthouse, and is 29 miles west of the Golden Gate.

Fassett, J. F.; has been at the S. F. bar since Sept., 1882; he was born in Wyoming Co., Pa., March 15, 1856; was educated at the University of Iowa, and admitted to the bar in Des Moines, in that State, July 20, 1882.

"Fast Mail Train," from N. Y. City, arrived June 4, 1876, with Jarratt & Palmer's theatrical company, and guests; time across the continent 84 hours, lacking a few seconds.

Fatal Leaps: Martin, a Frenchman, insane from drink, leaped from the roof of the Exchange Building on Battery street, opposite the P. O., Jan. 16, 1859.

A fatal leap from the balustrade of the interior Court of the old City Hall, upon the brick pavement below was made by Joel White, insane, aged 21, April 25, 1859.

Madame Augustine Simeon, proprietress of the Hotel de la Fraternité, at No. 225 Kearny street, leaped from the roof of an adjoining two-story building to the ground, and died in a few hours, July, 18, 1863.

Andrew Bohn, an aged Frenchman, jumped from the roof of a four-story building at the corner of Fourth and Howard streets, on the afternoon of March 27, 1897, and was picked up a moment later, dead and frightfully mangled.

Fell, Edward L.; an enterprising builder and street contractor, after whom Fell street was named, died of typhus fever, Dec. 4, 1864.

Felton, Chas. N.; pioneer of Sept., 1849; Assemblyman from San Mateo Co., 1880-81; Member of the lower house of Congress, two terms, March 4, 1885-March 4, 1889; U. S. Senator, elected March 19, 1891, in place of George Hearst, deceased; term ended March 4, 1893.

Felton, John B.; distinguished lawyer, whose professional career began and ended in S. F.; was born in Mass., in 1827; died at Oakland, Cal., May 2, 1877; delivered the oration at the dedication of the Mercantile Library building on Bush street, June 18, 1868. His interesting life is the subject of the Third Chapter of "Bench and Bar in California."

Female Dress; a Convention of 150 women assembled to consider the question of reform in woman's attire, April 6, 1874.

Ferguson, Clement; for his contribution to the history of California, see State Register for 1859.

Ferral, Robert; prominent lawyer; a journalist's son, and himself a journalist for many years before and after his admission to the bar, which took place at Aurora, Nev., in 1863; he located in S. F., first in June, 1852; was Chief Clerk of the Assembly, 1869-70; Secretary of the Senate, 1871-72; Chief Clerk of the Assembly again, 1875-76; Assistant District Attorney of S. F., 1874-75; Judge of the City Criminal Court, 1876-79; and Judge of the Superior Court, 1880-84. He was born in Philadelphia, on Oct. 13, 1841.

Fidelity Bank closed its doors on Nov. 12, 1877.

Field, Stephen J.; distinguished jurist; Justice of the Supreme Court of the United States since March 16, 1863, was appointed from California; arrived at S. F., Dec. 28, 1849; opened a law office, but within three weeks removed to Marysville. His long career is the subject of a thrilling chapter in "Bench and Bar," 1889; he was since assaulted by ex-Supreme Judge David S. Terry, in the dining hall of the railroad station at Lathrop, Cal., and his assailant was immediately shot and killed by David Neagle, U. S. Deputy Marshal, Aug. 14, 1889. Judge F. delivered the address at the Centennial of the Federal Judiciary at N. Y. City, Feb. 4, 1890.

Fifield, Wm. H.; prominent and industrious lawyer, of Boyd and Fifield (1889-91, Cope, Boyd & Fifield), was born in Mich., Feb. 8, 1843; and is a graduate of the Michigan State University, of the class of 1865; was admitted to the bar in that State in 1866, and has followed the profession in S. F. since Oct., 1868.

Filibusters; 240 in number sailed from S. F. in the bark Anita, to join Gen. Wm. Walker in Lower California, Dec. 13, 1853.

Findla, James; wealthy citizen; a pioneer of Oct. 1, 1847; sold to Thos. H. Blythe in 1850-51, the Market and Geary streets lots which made B. a millionaire; kept a coal yard at N. E. Pine and Battery streets until 1863; registered as a voter, Oct. 13, 1869, as born in Scotland, aged 57, and naturalized in Lafayette Co., Mo., in 1843; he died in France in 1895.

Mrs. Findla died in Paris, France, April 23, 1887, aged 75.

Finn, John F.; Superior Judge from Jan., 1880 to Jan., 1893, was elected three times—in 1879, drawing a short term ending in Jan., 1881; in 1888, for a full term of six years; and again in 1886, for a full term. The proceedings in the great Blythe estate and in the Sharon divorce case were begun before him, but were soon trans-

ferred to other departments of the Superior Court; he was defeated on the Republican ticket for Justice of the Peace, in 1869,
and was Attorney for Public Administrator Quarles in 1867-68,
and a part of 1866; he registered July 13, 1867, as born in the
island of Cuba, aged 28.

Fires: The first great fire in S. F. was on Dec. 24, 1849; it destroyed nearly all the buildings in the block between Kearny, Washington,
Montgomery and Clay streets; the loss was about $1,000,000; there
was no organized fire dep't at that day.

The second great fire was on May 4, 1850; the loss was about
$4,000,000.

The third great fire was on May 14, 1850; loss, about $5,000,000;
nearly every building and almost all the merchandise were destroyed between Clay and California streets from Kearny to the
water front. The burned district was entirely rebuilt within 60
days thereafter.

The fourth great fire was on Sept. 17, 1850; nearly all the
buildings were destroyed between Montgomery, Washington, Dupont and Pacific streets; they were cheap structures; loss, about
$500,000.

The fifth great fire was on May 4, 1851; about 2,000 buildings,
covering 18 squares, were destroyed, including many that were
supposed to be fireproof; loss, over $10,000,000; several lives were
sacrificed.

The sixth great fire was on Sunday, June 22, 1851; 14 blocks
were burned over, in 4 hours; loss, over $3,000,000.

The seventh great fire was on Oct. 23, 1863; all improvements
on the block between California, Sacramento, Davis and Drumm
streets, were consumed; loss, about $300,000.

Fire on the N. W. corner of Post and Stockton streets, destroyed the Occidental Skating Rink, and damaged near buildings,
Oct. 5, 1871.

The Pacific Wood Preserving Works were destroyed, Nov. 5,
1871; loss, $20,000.

J. Y. Wilson & Co.'s Pork Packing House was consumed, April
1, 1872.

Richardson & Holland's Planing Mill was destroyed May 15,
1872.

Improvements on Drumm street, worth $50,000, were consum-
ed, July 4, 1872.

Hayes Park Pavilion was destroyed Nov. 29, 1872; loss,
$60,000.

Pacific Wood Preserving Co.'s Works, on Berry street, were
again destroyed, Dec. 18, 1872.

Sage's Warehouse, containing 10,000 cases of coal oil, was
burned, Feb. 10, 1873.

Judson & Shepard's Candle Factory was burned June 16, 1873;
loss, $50,000.

Wm. J. Heney & Co.'s furniture establishment was damaged in $50,000, Nov. 25, 1873.

Atlantic Hotel was destroyed Dec. 1, 1873; a man named Adams perished.

Allyn & White's, Schultz & Van Bergen's, and other large houses, were consumed, July 10, 1874.

The Morocco Manufacturing Co.'s establishment, and the tannery of Geo. Griffin, were burned, July 12, 1874.

The Eureka Hair Manufactory was destroyed, Aug. 30, 1874.

The Alhambra building was badly damaged, March 22, 1875.

The University Mound College building was destroyed, April 4, 1875.

Fire in the vicinity of Fourth and Berry streets caused a loss of $75,000, May 9, 1875.

The Chemical Works at South S. F., were destroyed, July 15, 1875.

Fire in the Brittan building, corner of California and Davis streets, caused a loss of $250,000, May 25, 1876.

The Bay Sugar Refinery was burned June 9, 1876; the loss was $500,000.

The press rooms of the Bulletin and Call were injured to the extent of $5,000, June 11, 1876.

Nearly all the buildings in the block bounded by Third, Fourth, Brannan and Townsend streets, including several mills, manufactories, and the German Hospital, were destroyed, Aug. 28, 1876; loss, $500,000.

Sol. Wangenheim & Co.'s pickle factory was destroyed; loss, $10,000, Sept. 3, 1876.

The Capital Flouring Mills, on Sacramento street near Davis, were burned, Dec. 14, 1876.

The steam schooner, Pearl, was burned at Larue's wharf, Feb. 6, 1877.

The Lick House was damaged to the amount of $30,000, July 22, 1877.

Incendiary fires, by anti-Chinese rioters, damaged the great lumber yards at the city front, south of Market street, to the amount of $100,000, July 25, 1877. There followed many suits against the City, which had to make full reparation.

The Bancroft Building on Market street, running back to Stevenson street, was nearly destroyed by fire in 1886.

Fire Alarm and Police Telegraph was established on April 24, 1865.

Fire Department; Act to establish a Paid Fire Dep't was approved March 2, 1866; such Dep't being organized in December following.

Fireman's Fund Insurance Co.; a history of this oldest local insurance Co. is in "Resources of California" for Sept., 1886.

"Fireman's Journal," weekly newspaper, devoted to the interests of fire and military organizations, was established by Chase & Boruck, April 7, 1855.

Firemen's Jubilee, with a grand procession, city and country fire companies being in line, with their engines, occurred in June 17, 1861.

Fire Patrol was established in May, 1875, by the Board of Fire Underwriters.

Fire Insurance Patrol began active duty, May 24, 1875.

Firebaugh, H. C.; prominent lawyer; is a native of Ohio, a graduate of
Michigan University (Law Dep't) 1869, and has been at the S. F.
bar since 1876. In 1885-86, Mr. F. was a Member of the Assembly.

First Book published in California; death of the author, Dr. F. Wierzbicki,
occurred at S. F., Dec. 26, 1860.

First Child of civilized parents born in S. F., was Rosalie, daughter of
Jacob P. Leese, born April 15, 1838.

First Constitutional Election—on the adoption of the constitution framed
at Monterey, and for City and State officers—occurred Nov. 13,
1849.

First Execution of a person, pursuant to the sentence of a Court, was that
of José Forni, who was hung on Russian Hill for the murder of
José Rodriguez, Dec. 10, 1852.

First Flour Mills built in S. F. were the Commercial, built by Samuel
Grosh, in Aug., 1855.

First National Bank of San Francisco was organized in Oct., 1870.

First Postmaster at S. F., John W. Geary, arrived with the first regular
mail from the Atlantic States, on the steamship Oregon, March
31, 1849.

First Fire Insurance Co. established in S. F. was the San Francisco Insurance Co., March 20, 1861; E. W. Burr, President; C. O. Gerberding,
Vice President; Geo. C. Boardman, Secretary.   Mr. Boardman became President in 1863; the company went into liquidation in
1869. Philip McShane, manager of the Occidental Hotel, acting
as Secretary and Agent.

First Survey of S. F. was made by Capt. Juan Vioget in 1839, by order of
Gov. Alvarado, and covered the area bounded by Montgomery,
Dupont, Sacramento and Pacific streets.

Fisher, George; Consul for Greece; died June 11, 1873; a native of Hungary,
aged 78.   His life is the subject of a long article in the Bulletin
of June 18, 1873.

Fisher, Luther P.; veteran newspaper and advertising agent; has been
established in that business in S. F. continuously since 1855, residing always in Oakland.

Fisk, Asa, who had acquired a fortune of half a million dollars by money
lending in small sums upon notes with collateral security, died
March 5, 1897; a native of Mass., aged 78.

Fiske, Dr. H. M.; distinguished physician; a School Director at S. F.,
1878-79 and 1882; member Board of Health, 1889-91; died of paralysis, April 4, 1896, aged 72; native of Mass.

Fitch, Benjamin F.; brother of Wm. S. and G. K. Fitch of S. F., died at
Louisville, Ky., July 29, 1879, aged 39.

Fitch, Geo. H.; well-known journalist, and correspondent for the great
eastern dailies, has been connected with the S. F. Chronicle con-

GEORGE HAMLIN FITCH.

HISTORICAL ABSTRACT. 95

tinuously since 1880; registered on July 23, 1896, as born in N. Y., aged 43. He is a graduate of Cornell University, and attended the S. F. public schools in his boyhood.

Fitch, Geo. K.; veteran newspaper publisher and editor; was appointed State Printer by Gov. John McDougal on May 2, 1851; a full statement of the contest for that office between him and Eugene Casserly, is in first vol. of the California Supreme Court Reports, page 520; Mr. F. published the "Times and Transcript" at Sacramento, 1852-53; published with Thos. Rutherford, the "Prices Current and Shipping Lists" at S. F., for several years until towards the close of 1859, when he became one of the proprietors of the Bulletin; purchased, with Loring Pickering and J. W. Simonton, the S. F. Call, in 1870; sold his interests in Bulletin and Call, Jan. 10, 1895; registered May 14, 1867, as born in N. Y., aged 4♥.

Fitch, Henry S.; brother of Geo. K. Fitch; died at Washington, D. C. (whither he had removed from S. F. and became a well-to-do real estate operator, April 8, 1896; registered at S. F., Sept. 29, 1868, as a native of N. Y., aged 47.

Fitch, Thomas; an orator ranking next to E. D. Baker; born in N. Y. City Jan. 27, 1838; came to California from Wisconsin in 1860; stumped the State for Lincoln in that year; was Assemblyman from El Dorado in 1863; Member of the Constitutional Convention of Nevada in 1864; District Attorney of Washoe Co., 1865-67; represented that State in the lower house of Congress, 1869-71; practiced law in S. F., 1874-78; stumped the State for Greeley in 1872; has been residing in Arizona since 1878; was a Member of the Arizona House of Representatives in 1879. Among his public addresses, which are masterpieces of eloquence, are his Remarks to Sunday School scholars after their Floral Procession in S. F., July 4, 1861; address at dedication of Red Men's Hall, June 17, 1875; oration, July 4, 1875; oration, Memorial Day, 1876; all appearing in the local press; and his oration on Garfield, at Tombstone, A. T., Oct., 1881, a glowing extract from which may be found in the San José Mercury of Oct. 13, 1881. Mr. F. fought a duel near Virginia City, Nev., in 1865, with the poet-editor, J. T. Goodman, receiving a ball in his leg, which nearly ended his career. His home is now at Phœnix, Arizona (Fitch & Campbell)

Fitch, Thomas, Jr.; son of the preceding, was born in S. F., Nov. 30, 1862, and followed the business of a commission broker in S. F. in 1891.

Fitzgerald, O. P.; distinguished Methodist clergyman; Sup't of Public Instruction, Dec., 1867-Dec., 1871; was defeated for the same office by Henry N. Bolander (Rep.), Sept., 1871; was again defeated for that office, by Ezra S. Carr, (Rep.) in Sept., 1875; was editor of Fitzgerald's Home Newspaper, 1878-79; Chaplain of the Assembly, and a Committee Clerk, 1878; removed from the State in 1880; while editor of the Christian Advocate, at Nashville, Tenn., in May, 1886, he was defeated for Bishop of the Methodist Church

South, but at the General Conference of that Church at St. Louis, on May 19, 1890, he was elected a Bishop. He was born in N. C., Aug. 24, 1829.

Fitzgerald, Michael J.; a famous marine reporter for the S. F. Merchants' Exchange; became assistant to marine reporter H. C. Hoyt, in the spring of 1883, and was promoted to Hoyt's place, on the latter's death, in 1885. Mr. F. was born in Ireland in 1861, and came with his parents to S. F. in early boyhood.

Flanagan, Thaddeus; President of the United Ireland Branch of the Irish National League, died Sept. 11, 1885, a native of Ireland, aged 51.

Flavin, Martin J.; proprietor of the I. X. L. clothing house since 1874, died suddenly July 15, 1893; a native of Ireland, aged 46.

Fletcher, J. A.; a lawyer who was once law partner of Daniel Webster, and for whom it is said the statesman named his son Fletcher, removed from Boston into Northern California in the Fifties; located at S. F. in 1863, and died Feb. 15, 1873, aged 59; he registered as a native of Vt. See the strange case of Fletcher vs. Judge Daingerfield, 20 Cal., page 427.

Flint, B. P.; head of large wool houses since 1873, was a School Director, appointed Oct. 9, 1889, vice W. F. Goad, resigned, and served to the close of 1890. He was the Republican candidate for Mayor in 1879, and was defeated by Isaac S. Kalloch, nominee of the then powerful Workingmen's Party.

Flint, James P.; senior member of the pioneer shipping and commission house of Flint, Peabody & Co., died at Oakland, March 8, 1873, aged 71. He had kept his residence in Boston until 1864.

Flint, Wilson; whose vote in the legislature of 1856 prevented the election of Henry S. Foote to the U. S. Senate, was State Senator from S. F., 1855-56. (See Bench and Bar, pages 81-82.) He was wont to refer to the people of S. F. as "the noblest constituency on God's earth." Removed to Sacramento in 1859, and engaged in agriculture. For the violent assault upon him by Richard C. Barry in the Senate Chamber, May 7, 1855, see Senate Journal of that session, page 852. Mr. F. died in 1866. He was a pioneer of Dec. 28, 1849.

Flint, Peabody & Co., commission merchants, began business in 1849; they erected the warehouses in the block bounded by Battery, Sansome, Filbert and Greenwich streets, in 1854.

Flood, James C.; senior member of the Bonanza mining firm of Flood, O'Brien, Mackay & Fair, was born at N. Y. City, Oct. 25, 1826; died at Heidelberg, Germany, Feb. 21, 1889; he was a pioneer of Oct. 18, 1849; before going on the journey which was ended by his death, Mr. F. resigned the presidency of the Nevada Bank of S. F., Sept. 13, 1887, Jas. G. Fair succeeding him; he had, on Aug. 16th, executed a power of attorney to his son, Jas. L. Flood, giving his vast possessions into the latter's absolute control. On April 6, 1883, J. C. Flood paid to the trustees of the estate of James Lick, $400,000, for the lot on the westerly corner of Market and Fourth streets,

on which the Flood Building was erected a few years later. Mr.
Flood was in the habit of making large donations every Christmas
to the various Charitable Societies and Orphan Asylums; he sub-
scribed $25,000 to the Irish Famine Fund, Feb. 10, 1880. His estate,
amounting to many millions of dollars, was administered in San
Mateo County.
Mr. Flood's widow died at S. F., in Jan., 1897.

Flood, James L.; son of the preceding; became Attorney-in-fact of his
father, Aug. 16, 1887; of his mother, May 14, 1888; he became a
director of the Nevada Bank of S. F., in place of his father resigned, May 17, 1888; and President of the Bank in 1889; he has resided at Menlo Park since 1880.

Flood of 1861-62; Platt's Hall was fitted and arranged for receiving and
providing for the Sacramento sufferers, Jan. 15, 1862; the legislature adjourned at Sacramento, and convened in S. F., in the building on Battery street, opposite the Custom House, Jan. 24, 1862.

Flood at Marysville; a committee of S. F. citizens collected $15,000, and
sent it to the relief of the sufferers, Jan. 22, 1875.

Floods in France; French residents held a mass meeting and raised funds
to relieve the sufferers, June 30, 1875; $7,800 was remitted July
22, 1875.

Floral Procession of Sabbath School Children occurred on July 4, 1861;
beautiful words were spoken to them by the great orator, Thomas
Fitch. See "Fitch, Thomas."

Flores, Mrs. Magdalena, who was born in S. F. in 1840, of an influential
native family, before the American occupation, died at S. F., at
No. 28 Hinckley Alley, Dec. 18, 1896.

Floyd, Capt. Richard S.; respected citizen; President of the Lick Trustees,
died at Philadelphia, Pa., Oct. 17, 1890. When the war of the Rebellion broke out, he was a cadet at the Naval Academy at Anna-
polis, and he enlisted on the Confederate side, serving on the pri-
vateers Florida and Alabama; at the close of the war he came to
S. F. and found employment in the P. M. S. S. Co., becoming
commander of several of their steamers. He married the daughter
of the wealthy ex-Judge of the Supreme Court, Henry A. Lyons.
The carrying out of the Lick Trust relating to the construction of
the greatest observatory of the world on Mount Hamilton, was
largely due to Captain Floyd's skill and management. He was
born in Georgia in 1843.

Foard, J. Macdonough; one of the founders of the "Golden Era" weekly
in 1852, was born in Maryland, arrived in California in 1849; parted
with his interest in the "Era" in 1860, and with five others established the Sunday Mercury in 1861. Was a School Director,
1883-84; died Jan. 15, 1892.

Folger, Capt. Francis B., a prominent merchant, pioneer of Aug., 1849,
died May 21, 1862.

Folger, Capt. S. M.; died Feb. 12, 1897; native of Mass., aged 83; was
father of Mrs. Thos. B. Shannon.

Folsom, Capt. Joseph L.; pioneer of March 26, 1847, whose name was given to Folsom street, died in Santa Clara Co., Cal., in July, 1854. His will is printed as a form in Belknap's Probate Practice; 309 city lots belonging to his estate, were sold Jan. 10, 1856, realizing $607,695. See "Duels."

Foltz, Mrs. Clara S.; a widely known lawyer; was admitted to the bar of the District Court at San José, Sept. 5, 1878. She practiced law at S. F. until 1895, when she removed to N. Y. City. Mrs. F. is a sister of the prominent lawyer, Samuel M. Shortridge, and of Mr. Chas. M. Shortridge, proprietor of the "Call." A sketch of Mrs. Foltz's life is in the Post of Aug. 12, 1882.

Having been denied admission to Hastings College of the Law, because of her sex, Mrs. F. brought the question before Judge Morrison of the Fourth District Court, who decided in her favor. The Directors of the College appealed, and the Supreme Court sustained Judge M., saying that "the Directors were not justified in rejecting an applicant for admission as a student in the College, on the sole ground that the applicant was a female." (Foltz vs. Hoge, 54, Cal., 28.) The lady, however, did not take the college course, but was afterwards admitted to the bar of the Supreme Court, upon examination. That tribunal had admitted women to the bar before, as in the case of the wife of the attorney, John N. Young. (See "Young, John N.")

For the case of Mrs. F. against Dr. Henry D. Cogswell, for a $5,000 fee, see local papers of March 13, 14, 1888.

Miss Trella, daughter of Mrs. F., and Dr. Chas. G. Toland of S. F., were married at San Diego, Cal., Oct. 21, 1888.

Foote, Henry S.; distinguished lawyer and statesman; was born in Va., Feb. 29, 1804; after being U. S. Senator from Miss., he resigned the Governorship of that State in 1853, and came to California; was defeated for the U. S. Senate by the defection of Wilson Flint, a Senator from S. F., in 1856; removed in 1857 to Nashville, Tenn., where he died in May, 1880.

Foote, Henry S.; prominent lawyer; son of the preceding; was born in Miss., Oct. 13, 1840; admitted to the bar in Tenn., in July, 1860; came to S. F. in 1854; was afterwards educated at Georgetown College, D. C.; returning to Miss., held the offices of Justice of the Peace, Probate Judge, and District Attorney; was a Major in the Confederate army; located permanently in S. F., Jan. 1, 1883; was a Supreme Court Commissioner, 1886-91; U. S. District Attorney, by appointment of President Cleveland, since 1894. Mr. F. was appointed a Regent of the University of California by Gov. Markham, in May, 1892; his term will end in 1900.

Foote, Lucius H.; who has published more or less in prose and verse, and is not unknown in the world of letters, was born April 10, 1826, at Winfield, Herkimer Co., N. Y.; educated at Knox College, Ill., and at Western Reserve College, Ohio; arrived in California in the fall of 1853; admitted to the bar in 1856; Justice of the Peace,

Sacramento, 1856-57-8; Police Judge, Sacramento, 1859-60; Collector of the Port of Sacramento, appointed by President Lincoln, 1861-62-3-4; Adjutant General California, 1872-73-4-5; Delegate to the Republican National Convention, 1876; located in S. F., 1876; U. S. Consul at Valparaiso, Chili, 1877-80; U. S. Minister to Corea, 1881-83; Treasurer of California Academy of Sciences, and Secretary of its Board of Trustees, since 1891.

Foote, Wm. W.; distinguished lawyer; was born in Miss., Jan. 16, 1846; his father was elected to the U. S. Senate on the same day. Mr. F. came to California first in 1856; he fought in the war of the Rebellion in the Confederate army, being several times wounded and captured; graduated from the University of Virginia, and, after a short journalistic career in Omaha, Neb., came to California in 1869.

Forbes, Alexander, acquired a fortune in California prior to the discovery of gold; died in London, England, in 1863. See Bulletin, Jan. 9, 1864.

Forbes, Andrew B.; a prominent citizen, and pioneer of Oct. 10, 1849; was of Forbes & Babcock, agents of the Pacific Mail S. S. Co., from the beginning down to 1863; then held that agency alone until 1865; in 1866-67, was Superintendent of Wells, Fargo & Co.'s Bank; was Assistant Agent of the Pacific Mail S. S. Co. in 1868-69; General Agent of the Widows and Orphans Life Ins. Co., of N. Y., 1870-73; and General agent of the Mutual Life ins. Co., of N. Y., from 1871 to date (1897); also General Agent Continental Fire Ins. Co., 1877-80; also General Agent Niagara Fire Ins. Co., of N. Y., and Commonwealth Ins. Co., of Boston, 1879-80. Was Supervisor of the Seventh Ward, 1871-72-3. Mr. Forbes registered July 16, 1866, as born in N. Y., aged 42. His son, Stanly, has been associated with him in the insurance agency since 1894. The splendid building of the Mutual Life Ins. Co., of N. Y., S. E. corner California and Sansome streets, was completed in 1893.

Forbes, Chas. H.; well-known lawyer; was born in Mich., Dec. 3, 1859; was educated at the Law School of Boston University, graduating with the degree of L. L. B.; admitted to the bar at S. F., in Jan., 1887; and has been in practice at S. F. since 1888.

Forbes, Jas. Alexander; was the principal witness against Castillero in the suit over the New Almaden quicksilver mine, at S. F., in 1858; on July 20th he testified that he had lived in California 29 years; in Santa Clara Valley 26 years, and had married a native California lady there, July 4, 1834. His cross-examination by A. C. Peachy was masterly, and his answers were prompt and showed his great ability. He had been British Consul in California in pastoral days. (See the printed record in five octavo volumes, in United States vs. Andres Castillero, San Francisco, 1861.)

Foresters of America; composed originally of seceding members of the Ancient Order of Foresters; Supreme Court was organized at Minneapolis, Aug. 15, 1889; Grand Court of California was organized Nov. 20, 1889.

Fort Point (since namedF ort Winfield Scott); building of was begun in 1854, on the site of a small Mexican fortification, called Fort Blanco.

Foulds, John E.; well-known lawyer; has been connected with the law department of the Central and Southern Pacific R. R. Cos. nearly all the period since 1876, prior to which year he was for a long time phonographer in that department; he was born in England in 1848; was admitted to the bar in 1876. From 1888 to 1891 he was associated in the law practice with Hon. Carroll Cook.

Fountain Convention—to encourage the erection of drinking fountains, and so lessen the necessity for visiting drinking saloons—was organized Jan. 8, 1874.

Fountain, Lotta; at the intersection of Market, Kearny and Geary streets, was presented to the city by Miss Lotta Crabtree, the popular actress, whose infancy and youth had been spent in S. F. It was completed in Sept., 1875, being formally accepted by Mayor Otis on Sept. 9th. The presentation speech was made by Henry Edwards, actor. M. Cronin was the contractor for the stone work, plumbing and paving, and placing the Fountain in position; Wyneken & Townsend were the architects, and E. P. Hutchins was the agent for Miss Lotta. The Fountain was cast in Philadelphia, and, as cast, cost $5,775. Mr. Cronin was paid $1,500, the architects $275, and the freight was $875. Total, $8,475.

Fourgeaud, Victor J.; eminent physician; pioneer of Sept. 23, 1847; Assemblyman in 1857; prominent member of the Academy of Sciences; died Jan. 2, 1875, aged 58; a native of S. C.

Fourgeaud, Ellen, widow of the preceding, died at S. F., March 7, 1883, aged 72. She came overland to California from St. Louis in 1846; was of high intellectual attainments; one of the first American women to come to California. Her funeral was from Trinity Episcopal Church.

Fowler, Wm. H.; was born in Illinois, Dec. 6, 1860; admitted to the bar at S. F., June 29, 1888, and has since been in law practice here.

Fox, Chas. N.; distinguished lawyer; Judge of the Supreme Court from July 1, 1889 to Jan., 1891; was born in Michigan, March 9, 1829; located at Redwood City, in Aug., 1857; was District Attorney of San Mateo Co. for five years from Nov., 1857; represented Alameda Co. in the Assembly, in 1880; has had his office in S. F. since 1864. See Chapter XXXIX, of "Bench and Bar in California."

Fox, Geo. W.; who has been practicing at the S. F. bar since 1885, was born in N. Y., Aug. 28, 1842; was a soldier in the war of the Rebellion, and was Mayor of Chipota, Kansas, in 1871.

Foye, W. R. S.; has been a resident of S. F. since 1885, when he removed from Sacramento, where he had long been a prominent and wealthy merchant. See "Huntington, Hopkins Co."

Franco-Prussian War: An enthusiastic meeting was held for the benefit of the French sufferers, Feb. 14, 1871; $11,561 was contributed.

News was received of the signing of a treaty of peace between France and Germany, Feb. 24, 1871.

There was a grand illumination by the German residents on March 21, 1871.

Large and imposing procession of Germans, with literary exercises at the City Gardens, March 22, 1871.

French residents met to raise money to help pay the indemnity to Germany, March 7, 1872; $12,000 was raised on that night.

A French Ransom Fair was held in Union Hall, May 6-11, 1872; $24,000 realized.

The French Ransom Fund amounted to $36,433, June 25, 1872.

Frank, Nathan H.; well-known lawyer, partner of Judge Milton Audros; was born in S. F., June 3, 1858; was admitted to the bar in N. Y. City, in May, 1879; was educated at the University of California, and at the Columbia Law School, N. Y. City; and has been at the S. F. bar since 1879.

Franklin, Lady, arrived by steamer St. Louis from Panama, Feb. 11, 1861.

Franklin, Stephen; Secretary of the Bank of California from its organization in July, 1864, died Jan. 16, 1890; an elder in the St. John's Presbyterian Church, and Secretary of the Presbyterian Theological Seminary; registered June 22, 1866, as born in N. Y., aged 35. He was reporter on the Mercantile Gazette in 1860-61; editor of that paper in 1861-63, residing at San José. The figures 35, opposite his age on the great register in 1866, are thought to be a printer's error, as his friends say he was over 70 at his death.

Mrs. Gertrude Atherton, the story writer and novelist, is a grand-daughter of Stephen Franklin. For a brief notice of Mrs. Atherton, see "Some California Writers," in The Californian Magazine for May, 1893. This talented lady was a Miss Uhlhorn, and was born in S. F. She is now a widow, with a daughter of twelve years, and resides in London, England. In the latest from her pen (before this publication), a review, in "Vanity Fair," she declares that "California is a personality, and about three fictionists have caught it—Bret Harte, Mr. Vachell, and myself." See Supplement.

Frazer, Thomas; an able and opulent Presbyterian divine; Professor of Systematic Theology in the Theological Seminary in the Eighties, has his home in Sonoma County; is the subject of a sketch in the Occident (Presbyterian organ), May 4, 1887. He was born in Scotland in 1819.

Frazer River Mines; Exodus to, occurred in the spring and summer of 1858; by the end of June, one fifth of the Fire Dep't and nine policemen had emigrated; Judge S. C. Hastings and Patrick Crowley had departed; many citizens sold their city homes to raise money with which to get away; 15,000 persons departed during the six weeks ending June 26, 1858; the fever received its first damper on the return of 200 of the gold seekers, by steamer Cortes, July 15, 1858.

Freelon, Thos. W.; prominent lawyer; pioneer of Oct. 12, 1849; Assistant District Attorney, 1868-71; Judge of the Municipal Court of Appeals, 1878-79; Judge of the Superior Court, 1880-82; died March

30, 1885; a native of Vt., aged 58; his funeral was from Trinity Episcopal Church, conducted by the Pioneers and Veterans of the Mexican War.

Freeman, A. C.; widely known author and compiler of law books; was born in Illinois, May 15, 1843; was admitted to the bar at Sacramento, in 1865; his first law book, a "Treatise on Judgments," appeared in 1873; various other works followed, and on the death of John Proffatt, he was engaged by the publishers of "American Decisions," his work beginning with vol. 12. (Sketch by O. T. S. in Evening Post, June 24, 1882.) He located in S. F. in 1885.

Freeman, Ben. H.; pioneer of Sept. 9, 1849; a prominent Mason; pursued the business of a stairbuilder for twenty-five years; Commissioner of the Fire Dep't Dec., 1870-Dec., 1873, and President of the Board, 1872-73; President of the Pacific Protective Association, 1869-70; died while visiting N. Y. City, Sept. 16, 1876; a native of Mass., aged 52; his remains arrived under Masonic escort, and reposed in state at the First Baptist Church, from which the funeral was conducted with Masonic rites, Oct. 22, 1876.

Freeman, Frank F.; well-known lawyer; was born at Sacramento, Aug. 13, 1859; was admitted to the bar at that city in Nov., 1884; was deputy State Librarian, 1882 to 1890; located in S. F. in April, 1890; has been since 1885 assistant editor of American Decisions, and of American State Reports.

Freeman & Co.'s Express was robbed of $9,865 in gold dust, Aug. 1, 1859; the Company's porter and a confederate had taken the dust on the wharf where the Sacramento steamboat landed; they were convicted of the felony.

Freeman & Co.'s Atlantic and Pacific Express was established in 1849, and continued to 1852; it was re-established May 16, 1855. In 1853-54 John M. Freeman established expresses in the principal cities and towns on the West Coast of South America.

Frederickson, Wm.; an artist, died by his own hand on the beach near the Cliff House, March 28, 1874.

Free Public Library was formally opened on the evening of the 7th of June, 1879, with an address by Mr. A. S. Hallidie.

Fremont, John C.; First Republican candidate for the Presidency, 1856; when Captain in the topographical engineers, U. S. A., he led a surveying and exploring party across the continent in 1845, arriving at Sutter's Fort, Dec. 10th; arrived at S. F. Jan. 20, 1846; elected U. S. Senator, Dec. 20, 1849, for the short term which expired March 3, 1851. For his overland explorations, see his long letter in Alta, Nov. 20, 1854; early California history is given in his evidence on the Morehead Claim, Bulletin, May 7, 1858. He visited the State in 1888, and on May 4th visited the big trees at Felton, for the first time since 1846; after being Governor of Arizona Territory for a short period, he died in N. Y., July 13, 1890.

French, Frank J.; prominent lawyer; was born in Maine, Nov. 4, 1837; arrived in California, April 12, 1860; admitted to the bar of the

Supreme Court in 1870; settled in S. F. in 1867; was Attorney for Public Administrator Leman, 1882; appointed School Director, April 13, 1892, in place of William Harney, deceased, and resigned Aug. 30, 1893.

French Communists; a banquet was given by French residents to Paschal Grousset and Francis Jourde, two of the French Communists who escaped with Henri Rochefort from New Caledonia, May 24, 1874.

French Residents celebrated the anniversary of Emperor Napoleon Third, by a military procession, high mass at the French Church, a national salute from the corvette Didenant, and a ball at Platt's Hall, Aug. 15, 1862.

French Savings and Loan Society (first of that title) was incorporated, Feb. 1, 1860. It suspended Sept. 18, 1878; its Director General, Gustave Mahé, died by his own hand on the previous day; a meeting of the depositors was held in Platt's Hall, Dec. 31, 1878; Judge Dwinelle, of the 15th District Court, declared the bank insolvent, and appointed ex-Governor F. F. Low receiver, Oct. 7, 1878; the Supreme Court set the appointment aside, Dec. 11, 1878; a stormy meeting of depositors was held Dec. 30, 1878; the directors did not decide to go into liquidation until Jan. 22, 1879. Just before that date a new bank with the same title was organized and the affairs of the old bank were turned over to the new.

Fretz, Capt. R. S.; of the banking firm of Fretz & Ralston, 1859, and Donohoe, Ralston & Co., 1862, died at Napa White Sulphur Springs, June 26, 1863.

Friedlander, Isaac; the "Grain King;" a man of large mind and heart, and a giant in physical stature; died July 11, 1878, a native of Oldenburg, aged 54; President of the Chamber of Commerce two terms, 1876-77; suspended business, April 4, 1877, with liabilities of over one million dollars; on July 23, 1877, he and Annis Merrill were elected Water Commissioners. For his great wheat deals, see financial column of the Bulletin, Sept. 19, 1887. Mr. Friedlander's estate was appraised at $348,440 on Sept. 17, 1878.

Frohling, John; of the early large wine house of Kohler & Frohling, was a resident of Los Angeles, and died there, Sept. 20, 1862, of consumption. Mr. Kohler purchased his interest in the house of the widow.

Fruit Growers organized a co-operative association on Jan. 11, 1876.

Fry, John D.; pioneer of Aug. 2, 1849; President California Safe Deposit and Trust Co. since 1883; his residence, N. W. corner Jackson and Franklin streets, was completed in 1872, at a cost of $40,000. He registered first as a voter on Sept. 23, 1868, as a native of Ky., then aged 50.

Frye, Cary H.; Brevet Brig.-Gen'l, U. S. A., died March 5, 1873, aged 60.

Fugazi, John F.; President of the Columbus Savings and Loan Society; senior member of Fugazi & Co., steamship and railroad agents since 1877; Notary Public since 1883; was born in Italy in 1838.

Fulton Foundry was established by Worth, Hyde & Field as a machine

shop, Sept. 8, 1855; style changed to Fulton Iron Works, Hinckley,
Hyde & Co. proprietors, July 2, 1856; from 1859 to 1878, Hinckley & Co., proprietors; 1879-95, Hinckley, Spiers & Hayes were
proprietors; in 1895 the name was merged in that of the Fulton Engineering and Shipbuilding Works, which had been
established with the same proprietors, in 1892. Mr. Daniel B.
Hinckley, who is Vice President of the company in 1897, is the
Mr. Hinckley who became a member in 1856. Mr. Daniel E. Hayes
entered the firm in 1863, and Mr. Jas. Spiers (now President) in
1877.

Funded Debt of the City, under the Act of May 1, 1851, exceeded $1,000,000.

HALL OF JUSTICE.

www.ingramcontent.com/pod-product-compliance
Lightning Source LLC
Chambersburg PA
CBHW030618270326
41927CB00007B/1219